SpringerBriefs in Criminology

SpringerBriefs in Criminology present concise summaries of cutting edge research across the fields of Criminology and Criminal Justice. It publishes small but impactful volumes of between 50-125 pages, with a clearly defined focus. The series covers a broad range of Criminology research from experimental design and methods, to brief reports and regional studies, to policy-related applications.

The scope of the series spans the whole field of Criminology and Criminal Justice, with an aim to be on the leading edge and continue to advance research. The series will be international and cross-disciplinary, including a broad array of topics, including juvenile delinquency, policing, crime prevention, terrorism research, crime and place, quantitative methods, experimental research in criminology, research design and analysis, forensic science, crime prevention, victimology, criminal justice systems, psychology of law, and explanations for criminal behavior.

SpringerBriefs in Criminology will be of interest to a broad range of researchers and practitioners working in Criminology and Criminal Justice Research and in related academic fields such as Sociology, Psychology, Public Health, Economics and Political Science.

More information about this series at http://www.springer.com/series/10159

Claude-Hélène Mayer

Combating Wildlife Crime in South Africa

Using Gelatine Lifters for Forensic Trace Recovery

Springer

Claude-Hélène Mayer
Department of Industrial Psychology and People Management
University of Johannesburg
Johannesburg, South Africa

Institute for Criminal Justice Studies
University of Portsmouth
Portsmouth, UK

ISSN 2192-8533 ISSN 2192-8541 (electronic)
SpringerBriefs in Criminology
ISBN 978-3-030-05890-6 ISBN 978-3-030-05891-3 (eBook)
https://doi.org/10.1007/978-3-030-05891-3

Library of Congress Control Number: 2018968597

This Springer imprint is published by the registered company Springer Nature Switzerland AG
The registered company address is: Gewerbestrasse 11, 6330 Cham, Switzerland

Plans to protect air and water,
wilderness and wildlife,
are in fact plans
to protect man.

Stewart Lee Udall,
US Secretary of the Interior, 1961–1969

To all the people
who fight for the life and survival
of the wildlife in Southern Africa.

Acknowledgements

I hereby extend my heartfelt thanks to Dr. Paul Smith. Paul has been my mentor and guide in my studies at the Institute of Criminal Justice Studies (ICJS) at the University of Portsmouth in Portsmouth, UK, where a previous version of this book was submitted as a Master Thesis in the study path Master of Science in Crime Science, Investigation and Intelligence. Thank you also for helping with the image processing of the gelatine lifters. It was a real pleasure to be part of this broader research project on wildlife crime at your institute.

Further, I would like to express my thanks to Blanchie, Lolo and Ecee for their interest in crime investigation, investigative methods and wildlife crime combat.

For her unbroken enthusiasm to format and edit this book, I would like to thank my friend and colleague Elisabeth Vanderheiden.

Finally, I would kindly like to thank Judith Newlin, my editor in criminology at Springer. I thank you for the guidance and support.

Introduction

Green criminology is a growing field of interest in crime sciences. Wildlife crime, as a subtopic in green criminology, is increasing globally, specifically in Southern African contexts. At the same time, global and local programmes, actions and law enforcement strategies to combat wildlife crime are gaining strength. Forensic trace evidence provides one useful method of law enforcement in combating wildlife crime.

This study uses contextualising theories of green criminology, wildlife and wildlife crime internationally and in South Africa on the one hand and refers to forensic trace recovery on the other hand. Thereby, it focuses on the practicability of the use of gelatine lifters in South Africa, their analysis and evaluation in local and global contexts to provide an example of green criminology in action.

Accordingly, the purpose of this study is to contribute to evaluating the functionality and performance of the forensic method of using gelatine lifters for forensic-enabled intelligence to combat wildlife crime. The main aim is to undertake experimental research—as part of a broader research project—to evaluate the use, suitability and performance of gelatine lifters for the visualisation and sequential processing of finger-, shoe- and footprints and environmental traces in South Africa. Whilst, in this book, the example of South Africa is chosen, the methods are implementable in other global contexts, such as in other African countries and other remote and rural areas in Asia or South America in which access to technology is restricted and wildlife crime is ripe.

Methodologically, the research uses a preliminary experimental case study approach (natural experiment within a field setting) by applying an experimental research design. Limitations and ethical considerations are addressed.

Findings show good results for traces taken by gelatine lifters for forensic-enabled intelligence within South Africa. This is of particular importance, since the gelatine lifters, including the traces taken, were sent to England for evaluation purposes. Findings show that gelatine lifters worked well under various environmental conditions, such as moderate and high temperatures, in shady and sunny places, in indoor and outdoor areas and on different surfaces, such as tiles, wood, plastic and stone (clear and dusty). Conclusions and recommendations for theory and practice in green criminology and wildlife crime combat are discussed.

Contents

About the Author

Claude-Hélène Mayer is an Adjunct Professor at the European University Viadrina in Frankfurt (Oder), Germany, and Senior Research Associate in the Department of Management at Rhodes University, in Grahamstown, South Africa. She holds Master degrees in Crime Science, Investigation and Intelligence from the University of Portsmouth in Portsmouth, UK, and in Cultural Anthropology from the Georg-August University, Göttingen, Germany. She further on holds Doctoral degrees in Cultural Anthropology (Georg-August University, Göttingen, Germany), in Management (Rhodes University, Grahamstown, South Africa) and in Psychology (University of Pretoria, Pretoria, South Africa). Her Venia Legendi is in Psychology with focus on Work, Organisational and Cultural Psychology, acquired at the European University Viadrina in Frankfurt (Oder), Germany.

Claude has published several monographs, text collections, journal articles and special issues in English and German on management and leadership issues, mental health and well-being, conflict management, mediation and transcultural management, shame and women in leadership. Her regional focus of research is anchored in Southern Africa, particularly Tanzania and South Africa. Since a few years, she has gained scientific research interest in crime science with special regard to green criminology and wildlife crime combat.

List of Figures

List of Tables

Chapter 1
Introduction

1.1 Chapter Preview

This chapter serves as an introduction to the study on combating wildlife crime in South Africa within the context of green criminology. A case study investigation into the use of gelatine lifters for forensic trace recovery is presented. It provides first insights into the topic through an introduction to the field of study. The book further guides the reader through the theoretical approaches of green criminology and wildlife crime (combat), the research methodology, problem statement, purpose, aims and contributions. Finally, an overview of the structure of this study is given and the chapter closes with a summary.

1.2 General Orientation to the Study

Green criminology is a research area in criminology which deals with the analysis of criminal offences leading to environmental damage and/or destruction (Schmidt, 2013; Lynch, Long, Stretesky, & Barrett, 2017). Thereby, green criminology includes topics, such as pollution crimes, withdrawal crimes, ecological additions and illnesses, overproduction and overconsumption, toxic towns and ecologically devastated communities but also wildlife crime, wildlife trafficking, smuggling and poaching (South, 2010; Lynch et al., 2017). Further, green criminology usually points towards environmental justice and the analysis of criminal acts and offences in the context of the environmental law. Based on the scientific findings of green criminology, green crimes are described and interpreted, and their occurrence is explained. Stakeholders addressing and combating green criminology and wildlife crime are strengthened, such as environmental social movements and environmental non-governmental organisations.

C.-H. Mayer, *Combating Wildlife Crime in South Africa*, SpringerBriefs in Criminology, https://doi.org/10.1007/978-3-030-05891-3_1

Although recently, Moreto and Pires (2018) have argued that wildlife crime should be viewed as an independent research field which falls into the category of environmental criminology, in this book, wildlife crime and its combat are viewed as subcategories of green criminology—supporting the classification of Lynch et al. (2017). This categorisation is based on the fact that that green criminology takes particularly the understanding of cultural, economic, political and social factors into account which influence and impact wildlife crimes (Brisman, South, & White, 2016; Lynch & Stretesky, 2014).

Wildlife crime is defined as the "illegal trade in animals and animal products" and has become a major global problem during the past decades (Wilson-Wilde, 2010, p. 221). Nellemann, Henriksen, Raxter, Ash, and Mrema (2014) describe the global situation regarding wildlife crime as an environmental crime crisis, referring not only to financial costs but also to the environmental and social impacts of global wildlife crime. According to Wilson-Wilde (2010), up to US$ 20 billion are spent per year on combating wildlife crime globally. However, resources allocated do not compare with what is needed: although wildlife crime has advanced to one of the major contemporary global crimes causing environmental damage based on the "crimes against nature" worldwide (White & Heckenberg, 2014), Eman, Mesko, and Fields (2009) criticise that green criminology is still a marginalised topic within the broader field of crime sciences and criminology.

Moreto and Pires (2018) emphasise that wildlife crime is driven by various interlinked factors, such as the global and local political economies, political motivation and rebellion, but also by cultural and traditional drivers. Further on, the up and down of wildlife crime and its combat are also interlinked with supply-demand markets, human-wildlife conflict and crime opportunity. The negative impacts of wildlife crime are not debatable: wildlife crime creates huge amounts of ecological costs (short-term and long-term), economic, human, public health and national security costs. Wildlife crime combat aims at decreasing these costs and at strengthening the legal frameworks nationally and internationally to improve trade regulation, criminal justice and interregional mechanisms to strengthen legal frameworks from improving coordination and cooperation on local, regional and global levels (UNDP, 2017).

International and interdisciplinary cooperation and coordination in combating wildlife crime are required on all three levels, since international organised wildlife crime is strongly associated with other areas of crime, such as illegal drug trade (South & Wyatt, 2011), as well as through strong local, regional and international networks. To fight the strong interlinkages of criminal networks, effective action requires tight collaboration and communication between investigators, forensic specialists, commitment of law enforcement agencies and governments and willingness towards international information exchange (Wilson-Wilde, 2010). This international information exchange—which leads to increase actions against wildlife crime and the operating networks—is increasing (UNDP, 2017).

Whilst wildlife crime increases across various countries and presents itself as highly sustainable (Ayling, 2013), an increase in criminological attention (UNDP, 2017), expressed in, for example, growing research activities in forensic trace recovery methods to combat wildlife crime internationally, can be identified

(Wellsmith, 2011; Moreto & Pires, 2018). In particular during the past two decades, forensic trace recovery methods have improved significantly (Morgan, Wilfshire, Parker, & Bull, 2006). However, according to Wilson-Wilde (2010), the development of forensic techniques and their application are still in the beginning stages. Therefore, more international, collaborative research and action is needed to combat the crime more effectively. Wellsmith (2011) emphasises that criminal studies in wildlife crime remain marginalised and receive comparably limited resources due to a lack of political and governmental impetus which is, not at least, expressed through problems of (law) enforcement. However, the UNDP (2017) report emphasises that in many countries laws and regulations to prevent, detect and penalise wildlife offences increase, provisions to punish wildlife and forest crimes grow, community engagement to prevent wildlife crime is promoted and financial support is heightened to create global and local awareness of disadvantages and dangers of wildlife crime and illegal trade in protective wildlife. In African countries particularly, wildlife legal frameworks provide for increasing penalties if wildlife crime offences are committed through corruption (UNDP, 2017).

This study is based in the South African context where wildlife crime has become a serious issue and an environmental threat (South African Development Community, 2015; South & Wyatt, 2011; Wyatt, 2009). South Africa's Kruger National Park, once known as a wonderful natural habitat for the "Big Five"—including the lion, the African elephant, the Cape buffalo, the African leopard and the rhinoceros (abbreviation rhino)—and its huge biodiversity, has recently become known as the world's most concentrated site of commercial rhino poaching (Lunstrum, 2014). Although there is an increasing trend in lethal militarisation which can be identified in South Africa's natural habitats, the so-called green militarisation (Lunstrum, 2014), there is still a need for collaboration using global and local networks to prevent and combat the crime through an increase in research, prevention measures and action. This study aims at addressing this need.

The book uses the example of combating wildlife crime in South Africa. It, however, provides an example which can be transferred to other global contexts, such as other African countries and other remote and/or rural areas in Asia or South America in which access to technology might be restricted in comparison to European countries.

1.3 Theoretical and Methodological Approaches

The two theoretical sections in this study refer, on the one hand, to an overview on forensic trace recovery and the use of gelatine lifters and, on the other hand, to a description of the South African wildlife context and the identification of the background of increasing wildlife crime. By exploring the forensic and the contextual determents of the study, the reader is provided with the background information to understand the need, the context and the findings.

From a theoretical perspective, the study is based within the context of green criminology studies, particularly within the field of environmental forensic studies—which are urgently needed (White & Heckenberg, 2014) to contribute to the combat of environmental and wildlife crime from a forensic trace recovery perspective. It is further anchored in the interdisciplinary field of crime science and green criminology, whilst including interdisciplinary perspectives from social and cultural sciences. It is argued here along the lines of Moreto and Pires (2018) that interdisciplinary approaches are needed to bridge the disciplinary gaps to increase a holistic knowledge, disciplinary-spanning insights and intercultural knowledge to combat international networks of wildlife crime effectively. At the same time, a crime-specific approach is needed, as shown through the emphasis on the context description and the focus on the South African context, to decrease wildlife crime within local and international contexts.

In terms of the research methodology, this study is anchored in a preliminary experimental case study research design within a qualitative research paradigm. Within the case study, the data collection process, the setting, samples and sampling procedures are described extensively to create an understanding of the context of the study.

1.4 Problem Statement, Purpose and Aim

Wildlife crime is increasing globally, specifically in South Africa. Although international networking and local actions to combat wildlife crime are increasing in strength, criminal networks operate flexibly and ruthlessly, and wildlife species, such as rhinoceroses and African elephants, are threatened to be extinct in only a few years.

This study forms part of a larger international research project which aims at combating wildlife crime through forensic trace recovery and international cooperation and which is based at the University of Portsmouth in England, UK.

The *purpose* of this study is based within the culture-specific context of wildlife crime in South Africa. It contributes to the evaluation of new forensic methods of DNA testing (see Moreto & Pires, 2018)—here through gelatine lifters—to combat the illegal trafficking of ivory and rhinoceros horn. It thereby facilitates improved forensic-enabled intelligence between stakeholders of new crime prevention and combat methods.

The primary *aim* of this research is to undertake experimental research to evaluate the use and suitability of gelatine lifters for the visualisation and sequential processing of fingermarks, DNA and environmental traces in South Africa.

The *secondary aims* connected to the primary aim are:

- Review of contemporary research
- Contextualisation of the use of gelatine lifters as current technology deployed to combat ivory and rhinoceros horn trafficking
- Testing of gelatine lifters within the South African context and evaluation of traces in England, UK
- Providing conclusions and recommendations for theory and practice

By following the aims, this study contributes to the increased contextual understanding of wildlife crime in South Africa, from local to global perspectives, and provides new contextualised information on the use of gelatine lifters, data collection and evaluation. Thereby it is emphasised that the use of gelatine lifters is not restricted to its use in South Africa only. This book rather promotes the viewpoint that combating wildlife crime needs the intensified cooperation of international forces, as well as regional and local actors to combat wildlife crime effectively. It is therefore of extraordinary importance for international counterparts to understand contexts, like South African contexts, to alter and adjust their combating strategies on local, regional and global levels.

1.5 The Structure of the Study

This study is divided into six chapters.

Chapter 1 builds the introduction and provides a first insight into the topic, the theoretical and methodological background, the research methodology and the justification of the study. The purpose, aims and contribution are presented, and a problem statement and structural orientation are given. Each chapter concludes with a chapter summary.

Chapter 2 provides information on the context of wildlife crime—and its combat—in South Africa. In this chapter, the theoretical framework of the study within green criminology is outlined.

Chapter 3 provides insights into the theoretical approaches of forensic trace recovery from a green criminology perspective, as they relate to challenges of international law enforcement and exploring the seizure and maximisation of forensic potential in terms of formal identification of extrinsic and intrinsic evidence.

Chapter 4 discusses the research methodology employed. It embeds the research into a research design, paradigm and approach and provides deeper insights into the research setting. Ethical considerations and methodological limitations of the study are presented.

Chapter 5 reports the findings of the study.

Chapter 6 includes the discussion of the findings with regard to the theoretical literature review and provides conclusions and recommendations for future theory and practice.

A reference list is attached.

1.6 Chapter Summary

This chapter constitutes a general introduction to the study and provides the reader with an orientation to theories, context and research methodology. It defines the purpose, aims and contribution and gives a structural overview.

Chapter 2 provides a discussion of the theories referred to.

References

Ayling, J. (2013). What sustains wildlife crime? Rhino horn trading and the resilience of criminal networks. *Journal of International Wildlife Law & Policy, 16*, 57–80.

Brisman, A., South, N., & White, R. (2016). *Environmental crime and social conflict*. New York: Routledge.

Eman, K., Mesko, G., & Fields, C. B. (2009). Crimes against the environment. Green criminology and research challenges in Slovenia. *Journal of Criminal Justice and Security, 11*(4), 574–592.

Lunstrum, E. (2014). Green militarization: Anti-poaching efforts and the spatial contours of Kruger National Park. *Nature and Society, 104*(4), 816–832.

Lynch, M. J., & Stretesky, P. B. (2014). *Exploring green criminology: Toward a green criminology revolution*. Farnham: Ashgate.

Lynch, M. L., Long, M. A., Stretesky, P. B., & Barrett, K. L. (2017). *Green criminology. Crime, justice and the environment*. Oakland, CA: University of California Press.

Moreto, W. D., & Pires, S. F. (2018). *Wildlife crime. An environmental criminology and crime science perspective*. Durham, NC: Carolina Academic Press.

Morgan, R. M., Wilfshire, P., Parker, A., & Bull, P. A. (2006). The role of forensic geoscience in wildlife crime detection. *Forensic Science International, 162*(1–3), 152–162.

Nellemann, C., Henriksen, R., Raxter, P., Ash, N., & Mrema, E. (2014). *The environmental crime crisis: Threats to sustainable development from illegal exploitation and trade in wildlife and forest resources*. Nairobi, Kenya: UN Environment Programme.

Schmidt, H. (2013). Ein grüner Zweig der Kriminologie. Überlegungen zur green criminology. *Kriminologisches Journal, 45*(4), 260–278.

South African Development Community. (2015). *Law enforcement and anti-poaching strategy*. Retrieved from: http://www.gaborone.diplo.de/contentblob/4715602/Daten/6225475/SADC_LEAP_FINAL.pdf

South, N. (2010). The ecocidal tendencies of late modernity: Transnational crime, social exclusions, victims and rights. In R. White (Ed.), *Global environmental harm: Criminological perspective* (pp. 228–247). Devon: William Publishing.

South, N., & Wyatt, T. (2011). Comparing illicit trades in wildlife and drugs: An exploratory study. *Deviant Behaviour, 32*(6), 538–361.

UNDP. (2017). *Strengthening legal frameworks to combat wildlife crime*. Symposium Report: Africa-Asia Pacific Symposium, Bangkok, 4–5 July 2017 – United Nations Inter-agency task force on illicit trade in wildlife and forest products. http://www.undp.org/content/undp/en/home/librarypage/environment-energy/ecosystems_and_biodiversity/strengthening-legal-frameworks-to-combat-wildlife-crime.html

Wellsmith, M. (2011). Wildlife crime: The problems of enforcement. *European Journal on Criminal Policy ad Research, 17*(2), 125–148.

White, R., & Heckenberg, D. (2014). *Green Criminology. An introduction to the study of environmental harm*. Oxon: Routledge.

Wilson-Wilde, L. (2010). Wildlife crime: A global problem. *Forensic Science, Medicine and Pathology, 6*, 221–222.

Wyatt, T. (2009). Exploring the organization of Russia Far East's illegal wildlife trade: Two case studies of the illegal fur and illegal falcon trades. *Global Crime, 10*(1–2), 144–154.

Chapter 2
The Context: Wildlife and Wildlife Crime in South Africa from a Green Criminology Perspective

2.1 Chapter Preview

This chapter is concerned with the theoretical frame of green criminology and the context of the research. It provides an outline and brief overview of wildlife and wildlife crime from a South African perspective, revising context-specific characteristics and challenges. It further discusses law enforcement on wildlife crime with regard to the continental and national context of this study. The chapter ends with a short summary.

2.2 Green Criminology Perspectives

The concept of green criminology was first introduced by Lynch in 1990, relating to environmental crimes and harms affecting human and nonhuman life, ecosystems and the planet as a whole (Brisman, 2014). Green criminology has since become a well-recognised field in criminology and is viewed as being particularly important when the perspective is fostered to understand the spatiotemporal and situation factors which influence environmental crime. It provides an inter- and multidisciplinary approach to combating environmental crimes, wider environmental harms, ecological justice and an ecological justice perspective (Nurse, 2017). Green criminology aims at exploring the cultural, the social, the economic and the political factors which impact on the crime and its combat (Beirne & South, 2007). It uses a contextual approach to explore and clarify the context of the crime and the various other factors which impact on the crime and its combat (Brisman, South, & White, 2016).

It has been debated if green criminology is a theory or if it contains a theory (Brisman, 2014). Brisman (2014) points out that green criminology and its definition always depend upon the used constructs researchers use to define a subject

C.-H. Mayer, *Combating Wildlife Crime in South Africa*, SpringerBriefs in Criminology, https://doi.org/10.1007/978-3-030-05891-3_2

and emphasises that green criminology consists of a strong interaction with other disciplines: green criminology is therefore a construct which is founded in intra-disciplinary approaches used in criminology and one that is founded in interdisciplinary approaches by drawing on social sciences, biology, environmental studies, sociology and cultural sciences. Brisman and South (2013, 2014) have even suggested a "green cultural criminology" which takes cultural criminology's concerns into consideration and which focuses on the interrelationship of culture and crime within the dynamic socio-economic and political contexts.

This study of green criminology further is embedded in interdisciplinary approaches, including a crime science perspective which is an applied crime-specific approach. This approach focuses on understanding the specific crime from a spatiotemporal and situational perspective of crime events, aiming at the goal of detecting and understanding crime and developing measures for preventive and reductive actions. Since crime sciences focuses on the crime and not on the individuals involved, it can be supportive in wildlife crime combat. This is particularly the case when it is empirically supported (Guerette & Bowers, 2009), as in this study.

2.3 Green Criminology and Wildlife Crime

Wildlife crime has been recognised as a core concern in green criminology (van Uhm, 2016; Nurse, 2015). Since the 1990s, Benton (1998) has pointed out that green criminology, within the ecological justice discourse, needs to address harms to the environment and nonhuman animals, and Lynch and Stretesky (2014) have emphasised their disappointment that criminology as a discipline does not take green harms seriously, particularly since green crimes constitute a major threat to human survival. Thereby, green criminology does not only focus on criminal law concepts but also considers justice, morals, victimisations and the impact of different organisations, such as non-governmental organisations and the state as a major contributor to environmental harm. It also follows the call of South (2010) to following new critical viewpoints and developing alternative ways of addressing environmental harms beside mainstream criminology. Hall (2017) further argues that a cultural perspective is needed to resolve conflict and to develop restorative justice systems with regard to environmental contexts and particularly with regard to nonhuman animal harms. Flynn and Hall (2016) further on emphasise that the rejection of exploring the topic of nonhuman victimisation is not longer conceptually and philosophically justified within the context of green criminology. This study at hand does not focus on nonhuman victimisation as such; however it aims at contributing to strengthen the focus on nonhuman animals in (green) criminology through the improvement of forensic trace recovery to minimise wildlife harm and crime. As according to von Essen and Allen (2017), it is proposed that wildlife crime, violence and victimhood are unjustifiable as a mode of political dissent and that green criminology and crime studies need to aim at developing effective measures of wildlife crime combat to support political justice.

Research has focused on and examined a variety of legal and illegal acts in wildlife crime, such as trafficking, consuming of wildlife and poaching, and researchers have applied criminological frameworks (Hübschle, 2016b; Moreto, 2016; Wong, 2016). According to Van Uhm (2018), green criminology has mainly focused on harm of wildlife crime as proscribed by law, situational crime prevention and ecological harm, applying new and alternative ways of focusing on wildlife prevention and crime combat. Cultural aspects and contextual question have received limited attention in (illegal) wildlife markets and its combat in local and global perspectives. Van Uhm (2018) provides a well-written overview on culture-specific interests in selected wildlife and animal parts, such as rhino horns which are, for example, attractive for the traditional Chinese market. Van Uhm (2018) argues for a green criminological-extended harm-based approach which rejects the conventional rather narrow definition of crime by orthodox criminology and which includes the sociocultural and historic constructions of crime within the context of wildlife crime and its combat. In the following chapter, the South African context will be presented and explored.

2.4 Wildlife and Context-Specific Perspectives in South Africa

When people think of African countries, they often think of wildlife. South Africa is one of the countries which are particularly rich in biological diversity, holding huge internationally recognised natural habitats (Cousins, Sadler, & Evans, 2010). Traditionally, these habitats have been known for high amounts of wildlife. Wildlife is defined as "protected wild animals" which are viewed as "common property" and fall under the Department of Environmental Affairs in South Africa (Snijders, 2015, p. 15).

Wildlife, its production and conservation and wildlife-based tourism are important economic lifelines for South Africa (Michel et al., 2006). However, Snijders (2015, p. 15) emphasises that in South African national debates, wildlife (and its protection) does not take a central role, as it does in other African countries, since it falls under the category of "non-listed species", environmental legislation and the "ambiguous realm of 'biodiversity'". In post-apartheid South Africa (since 1994), wildlife laws were hardly debated or readjusted. If they were adjusted, then only to a small degree, as in the context of poaching and animal rights (Snijders, 2015).

During the last few years, however, the need for conserving the natural habitats has been exclaimed increasingly in South Africa. This is due to the loss of biodiversity, the environmental destruction of natural environments, the habitat loss and the national and international problems regarding the protection of endangered species through encouraged poaching for subsistence and commercial activities (Ayling, 2013; Newmark & Hough, 2000).

Historically and during the apartheid years, white European immigrants in South Africa majorly ran wildlife and game farming. Snijders (2015) emphasises that this is currently still the case. Accordingly wildlife farming has become a highly debated political issue of the racially still "untransformed" South Africa, and activists try to integrate people from "previously disadvantaged South African cultural groups"[1] into the wildlife production and industry (The National Agricultural Marketing Council, NAMC, 2006). However, this proves to be a challenge and is rather a political attempt of racial transformation than a wildlife- and conservation-based approach to integrate cultural groups throughout the nation to conserve wildlife.

Wildlife parks in South Africa are often surrounded by local communities which mainly belong to these "previously disadvantaged groups" and are regarded as the most underdeveloped communities within South Africa. Recent policies aim at addressing the conservation of wildlife, whilst adhering to the socio-economic needs of the rural communities of national parks. Wildlife protection and conservation can thus only be tackled when socio-economic needs of local inhabitants are addressed as well (Tapela & Omara-Ojungu, 1999). The South African government (SA Government, 1996), therefore, aims at driving conservation and natural habitat protection by running programmes which support the sustainability of wildlife and the economic prosperity of rural communities to prevent poaching and to include members of previously disadvantaged groups in wildlife production (NAMC, 2006).

Besides these transformational changes, ownership issues regarding wildlife ranching in the South African context have also changed. During the past years internal constraints, such as funding shortages for public, have led to changes to the structure of land use and land ownership of governmental-owned parks. It seems as if privatisation and commercial production have become the foundations of wildlife and conservation (Ashley & Wolmer, 2003). In the post-apartheid era in South Africa, the racially based land dispossessions implemented during apartheid are challenged by new land reforms which allow members from previously disadvantaged groups to reclaim the land they were forcefully removed from during apartheid. The possibility to reclaim previously disowned land however often clashes with the defined conservation areas in South Africa. Claims target conservation areas which leads to conflict regarding conservation, land reforms and interests of individuals and groups involved (Kepe, Wynberg, & Ellis, 2005).

Furthermore, various externally initiated challenges, such as external market forces, migration due to irrigation shortages, etc., impact on the wildlife economy (Newmark & Hough, 2000). Therefore, wildlife ranches face impacts on the basis of a changing political, economic and natural environment. Based on these changes and political reforms, South African landowners have been granted to acquire full ownership over wild animals on their land (Snijders, 2012). According to Snijders (2012), one sixth of the country's total land is nowadays fenced for "game farming" and for wildlife-based productions which include live trade and hunting. South Africa owns the biggest wildlife industry on the continent (Damm, 2005).

[1] Previously disadvantaged groups include members of African, Indian and Coloured descent, women and individuals with disability.

At the same time, wildlife ranching has generally become a fast-growing, recognised agricultural enterprise, and private landowners and wildlife ranchers have increasingly invested into this agricultural industry (Reilly, Sutherland, & Harley, 2003). Besides many of the positive factors which drive private landowners to pursue game farming and wildlife ranching, landowners feel challenged, for instance, by the strong impact of the needs of the tourist industry on the economy, the need to drive conservation objectives and the managing of wildlife populations within their owned land (Cousins et al., 2010). They also feel threatened by a huge set of national regulations they have to abide to which leads to feelings of working in a pressurised work environment (Snijders, 2015).

Furthermore, wildlife ranching is affected by various drivers and constraints, such as global hunting patterns, climate change, veterinary disease control policies, translocation and taxation laws, as well as land reforms, poaching and human-wildlife conflict (Taylor, Lindsey, & Davies-Mostert, 2016) to which landowners have to adjust rapidly and flexibly.

Since the South African wildlife ranching industry has expanded their land for hunting purposes, the South African hunting industry is growing (Jones & Weaver, 2008), not least due to disruptions of hunting possibilities in other African countries through war, political instability, land reforms and increasing poaching and human expansion into wildlife areas and a broadening of the demand for hunting areas by US American, Chinese and Russian hunters (Taylor et al., 2016). The "neoliberalisation of nature", however, has been criticised extensively, and the trend in the treatment of nature is worrying (Büscher, 2013), especially when looking at the poaching crisis (Taylor et al., 2016).

Wildlife in South Africa is and will continue to be affected by climate change, including increasing temperatures, aridity and rising sea levels. This leads to a significant loss of biodiversity and African mammal species (Taylor et al., 2016). However, according to the authors, there is also an increase in threat to wildlife species due to spreading diseases which might result in an even larger loss of wildlife.

From the viewpoint of taxation laws and subsidies, wildlife farming is not subsidised in South Africa (Cloete, Van Der Merwe, & Saayman, 2015), and wildlife farmers are often threatened by land reforms of the South African government (DRDLR, 2011) which aims at deracialising the rural economy and redistributing the land. At the same time, wildlife ranchers are also criticised for denying local communities access to diverse resources by fencing land into private game reserves (Brockington, Duffy, & Igoe, 2008). This leads to an even larger polarisation and politicisation of the wildlife farming business which needs to be taken into account when explored in the context of increasing wildlife crime.

Finally, Taylor et al. (2016, p. 108) refers to the key risks experienced in wildlife ranching based on "poaching and human-wildlife conflict". According to the authors, South Africa finds itself in a poaching crisis:

> …the three most serious poaching issues at present are the rhinoceros poaching crisis, the African Elephant poaching crisis and poaching for the bushmeat trade. (Taylor et al., 2016, p. 108)

Recently, it has been pointed out that not only elephants and rhinos are in the spotlight of trafficking and extinction in South Africa anymore but that, for the first time in history, big wildlife cats are threatened due to lost habitats and disappearing prey (SABC, 3 March 2018). The problem of wildlife crime and its combat has been described from different perspectives (e.g. Ayling, 2013; Ramutsindela, 2016; Snijders, 2015) and will be addressed in the next subchapter on wildlife crime.

2.5 Wildlife Crime in South Africa

International wildlife crime and (cross-border) trafficking is often placed second in overall profitability, following the profitability of the illegal drug trade; however, it does not (yet) gain the same public and professional awareness (South & Wyatt, 2011). Wyatt (2009) reports that wildlife crime has advanced to the stage of organised crime which is defined by the United Nations (2008) as:

> a structured group of three or more persons, existing for a period of time and acting in concert with the aim of committing one or more serious crimes or offences established in accordance with this Convention, in order to obtain, directly or indirectly, a financial or other material benefit.

Wildlife crime and poaching in South Africa are in the hands of organised crime (Wyatt, 2009). Since 2010, poaching incidents in Southern Africa have tripled and thereby endanger species, threaten communities and undermine local economies (Institute for Security Studies, 2017). It has recently been pointed out that in the South African Development Community (SADC) countries, only around 351,000 elephants are still roaming, a species which is currently listed as "vulnerable as a result of poaching and illegal ivory trade" and habitat destruction (South African Development Community, 2015, p. 5).

Besides the vulnerable status of elephants, rhinoceroses have become an endangered species. Of the Northern white rhinoceros, there is only one population of four animals to be found in a private conservancy in Kenya. The Southern white rhinoceros is mostly located in South Africa with approximately 19,000 animals remaining (South African Development Community, 2015, p. 5). The black rhinoceros, which was once the most numerous in the world, has been reduced to only three species, living in Southern African countries. Altogether the white rhinoceros is estimated in terms of numbers of around 20,000 in total in the SADC countries, whilst the black rhinoceros has already been reduced to around 4500 (South African Development Community, 2015, p. 6–7). Scientists expect the white rhinoceros to be extinct in the year 2025 if the decrease in population continues (Ferreira, Botha, & Emmett, 2012; Martin, 2012).

South Africa is facing difficult times. Whilst there is a decrease in the total number of wildlife, there is at the same time a huge increase in more wildlife species being classified as endangered species through poaching of wildlife animals and wildlife crime in general (Dalton & Kotze, 2010). With the increase in wildlife crime, scientific research has grown within the South African context of security studies, criminology and terrorism (Ramutsindela, 2016), criminal networks (Ayling, 2013), illegal and legal markets of horn trading and transnational illegal wildlife trade (Harvey, 2016; Hübschle, 2016a; Warchol, 2004) and green militarisation (Lambrechts & Goga, 2016; Shaw et al., 2016), as well as categorisations of poachers (Eliason, 2008).

The discourse on wildlife population decline is not only related to subsistence purposes of the local inhabitants and the problem of marginalisation of the rural communities, as often referred to in the past (e.g. Lambrechts & Goga, 2016). It is also related to legal and illegal commercial purposes which are not only locally and nationally driven but which are internationally pursued and transnationally organised. However, it has been criticised that in the past very little research has focused on illegal hunting and a need for research to reduce wildlife crime in South Africa has been emphasised (Warchol & Johnson, 2011).

This study adheres to this exclaimed need and takes into account that horn and ivory are often transported through various African countries and are then shipped to international destinations. Therefore, traces, which are recovered in transit, often provide numerous trace and contact evidence from different sources. How these traces are dealt with is based on issues associated with law enforcement, the capability of the forensic science personnel and the availability of methods used to recover traces. These methods should be easy to use, robust and easy to protect. The demands regarding the material used for identification of traces show that there is a need to respond to these challenges. This can be achieved through support of front-line researchers and investigators in the countries aiming at protecting wildlife from being poached through improving the use of forensic processes and procedures. This leads to this initial pilot research to test gelatine lifters as a method to lift contact traces at source and examine the marks to establish the presence of identification materials and any forensic intelligence.

Research shows that, whilst poaching activities dropped in the 1990s, they picked up increasingly in the year 2000, increasing drastically in 2009 and peaking in 2013. This is indicated by the high numbers of large-scale ivory seizures for more than 500 kg (South African Development Community, 2015, p. 8). During the past years, poaching rates exceed natural population growth of elephants, as well as rhinoceros populations. Thereby, South Africa has been the country with the highest poaching rates on the continent (South African Development Community, 2015, p. 9). South Africa spends about 200 million rand annually and employs 450 rangers just to protect the wildlife in Kruger National Park (Institute for Security Studies, 2017). Latest figures show that the estimated 37 tonnes of rhino horn poached between 2010 and 2016 in South Africa were sized by law enforcement agencies (Institute for Security Studies, 2017)—however the number of undetected crime and unrecorded cases are not estimated but assumed to be high as well.

Biggs, Courchamp, Martin, and Possingham (2013), for instance, point out that rhinoceros poaching has increased significantly due to a strong demand for rhinoceros horn in countries of the Far East, such as China and Russia. In the near future, it is also expected that elephant poaching in South Africa will increase similarly to that of rhinoceros poaching (Wittemyer et al., 2014).

Besides horn hunting and poaching, reptiles, such as snakes, lizards, turtles, tortoises and crocodiles, have also been described as crime targets within South African contexts and are traded illegally (Herbig, 2010). Accordingly, numbers of reptiles are shrinking and many are critically endangered. However, according to the South African Development Community (2015, p. 11) poaching of ivory and horn does not necessarily increase due to a current demand but rather due to speculative stockpiling of ivory in China.

Many authors refer to the problem of the demand of East Asian markets with regard to horn, ivory and other high-value species for curios, luxury foods and medicine (Biggs et al., 2013; Challender, 2011). Authors emphasise a need for social marketing programmes to create awareness and reduce the demand on the Chinese market (Challender & MacMillan, 2014). However, Lambrechts and Goga (2016) emphasise that it is incorrect to blame "the other", which are here the Asian crime groups, for the increasing poaching problem, since this would strengthen the view on "the criminal as an outsider from society" which is a well-known phenomenon in criminal sciences (Lambrechts & Goga, 2016).

Besides the phenomenon of externalisation ("blaming the other") and the problem wildlife crime causes on political, economic and juridical levels, wildlife crime inherits further on the loss of the rightful cultural inheritance of the people of South Africa (Griffiths, 2017). Griffiths (2017) emphasises that in South Africa members of all ethnic and cultural groups are in the one or the other way socially and culturally connected to their wildlife. She argues that the impact of wildlife crime on South African inhabitants might be even seen as a form of cultural victimisation. The author, however, also explains that South Africans are often not aware of the loss of their natural heritage. This unconsciousness or unawareness might be related to the high poverty statistics in the country and the pressure of a majority of South African struggling to survive on an existential level (Griffiths, 2017). Duncker and Goncalves (2017) support the perspective due to the fact that they have studied the perception of wildlife crime within local communities. Their findings show that most of the community members are in favour of conservation only if they derive adequate benefit from it. They also found that community members are reluctant to being willing to stop, prevent or report poaching due to the perception that the parks do not act in favour of the communities (Duncker & Goncalves, 2017). Surely, the perspectives of local communities need to be taken into account seriously to create a sustainable future and project wildlife in South Africa. Hübschle (2017) supports the view of Duncker and Goncalves and adds that:

> instead of recognising the local people as important change agents in wildlife conservation, conservators are calling for more boots on the ground, helicopter gunships and new technologies.

This should, according to Hübschle (2017), change towards a community-based concept which takes the structural inequality within the country and as highlighted by Griffiths (2017) into account as a major factor in wildlife crime.

The wildlife poaching and the high demand of bushmeat purchases have put serious threats to wildlife in South Africa and have at the same time evoked an increase in security measures (Lindsey & Taylor, 2012). This need for an increase in investment in security in the wildlife industry already leads to the search for alternative land uses by landowners who consider withdrawing from game farming (Lindsey et al., 2013). However, the question remains as to what law enforcement in South Africa is doing to combat wildlife crime.

2.6 Law Enforcement on Wildlife Crime in South Africa

According to latest research in poaching and wildlife crime (Lambrechts & Goga, 2016), it is expected that poaching will continue to grow. The authors emphasise the flexibility of the organised crime groups, the lack of legitimacy by the South African state, the growing demand of products and market size and the involvement of various organised crime groups which makes it difficult to combat the crime. However, wildlife crime is also a very complex issue, and heated debates on legalisation of wildlife products in the context of corrupt states or the combat of the illegal trade are accompanying the discourse on law enforcement and wildlife crime (Bennett, 2015b; Harvey, 2016). One related core problem in the fight against wildlife crime is the explicit void in research regarding actors which bridge the legal and illegal market divide and the failed understanding of their behaviours and interrelations to develop functioning law enforcement measures and criminal justice interventions (Hübschle, 2016a).

However, various movements can be recognised in the South African context with regard to law enforcement and security measures in the battle against wildlife crime (Bennett, 2015a). These include discourses on legalising crime (Bennett, 2015b; Harvey, 2016), green militarisation movements (Shaw et al., 2016) and security coordination (Hübschle, 2016a). In the South African context, for example, the ESPU, an elite police unit, has been implemented to enforce conservation laws in South Africa on a practical level. Other movements aim at stopping corruption amongst the low-paid law enforcement officers (Warchol, 2004). Strategies, movements and operations range from individual, micro-levels, to organisational, meso-levels, and societal macro levels of implementation.

Law enforcement action has been taken on international, intercontinental, national and local levels, and "from 2009 through 2013, at least 77 large-scale ivory seizures occurred", indicating an increase in illegal trading of ivory and horn on a large-scale basis. Furthermore it provides evidence for the orchestration of transnational criminal operations on the one hand and improved law enforcement on the other hand (South African Development Community, 2015, p. 9).

In 2012, an Environmental Compliance and Enforcement Committee (ECEC) and Working Group were initiated internationally to assist Interpol to identify emerging patterns and trends in environmental crime enforcement (ECEC, 2015). Under these auspices, the Wildlife Crime Working Group has been built to combat wildlife crime, namely, poaching, trafficking or possession of legally protected flora and fauna.

In 2015, a law enforcement and antipoaching strategy for the years 2016–2021 has been released, in which an overview on the crime and international responses to combat wildlife crime are provided (South African Development Community, 2015). In this strategy paper, a policy framework and an assessment for SADC law enforcement are presented which is based on the identification of three factors which mainly contribute to the consistent increase in poaching. These include poverty at local levels, governance at national levels and the demand for illegal ivory at the global level (South African Development Community, 2015, p. 10).

Hübschle (2016a) points out that there is limited success in disrupting wildlife crime, although antipoaching measures and interventions on different levels, as well as campaigns to reduce the demand, are instituted. These measures and interventions include, for example, an action plan at the SADC and national levels to protect elephants. However, since its implementation (2005), the aims have not yet been reached (South African Development Community, 2015, p. 12). On international levels, a UN Convention on International Trade in Endangered Species has been released (CITES, 1973), and various international stakeholders in the USA and Europe, as well as international NGOs, have joined in the fight against illegal trade and wildlife crime.[2] These stakeholders aim at eradicating the market for illegal products, building international cooperation and strengthening law enforcement on micro-, meso- and macro-levels. On a continental level, African stakeholders have held several conferences and summits with regard to the topic and have released conventions on conservation of nature and natural sources.

However, some of the strategies and actions have been criticised strongly, as, for example, the CITES ban on the international trade of ivory—dealing with the "regulated" ivory market. The ban impacted negatively on the legal market, since sanctions were released for the states which do not comply with the CITES convention (Lemieuy & Clarke, 2009, p. 454). To CITES (2008) 173 states have agreed. They agreed on developing national legislation to provide a framework and funding to implement the international trade convention, involving agencies in data collection and law enforcement, reporting on the developments and measures taken. However, CITES does not address and prohibit the trade of ivory within countries, and unregulated markets do not have to register or provide proof that their ivory is not from poached animals (Lemieuy & Clarke, 2009) which leaves space on the one hand for tourists to buy ivory within their tourist destination, and on the other hand it opens doors for wholesalers buying within the countries to resell in other countries in Africa or Asia (Courouble, Hursh, & Milliken, 2003). This "unregulated" market is the responsibility of national policies and law enforcements and often stays unattended to. It, therefore, is one of the biggest threats to elephant populations in Africa, since CITES does not control domestic markets and therefore loses effectiveness with the ban on the international trade of ivory (Lemieuy & Clarke, 2009). Stiles (2004) finally concludes that the ban has led to some markets of ivory trade having declined, whilst others—particularly those with domestic markets—are growing.

---

[2] See South African Development Community (2015) and CITES (2015) for complete member/stakeholder lists.

The SADC Treaty (1999), as another approach to law enforcement and antipoaching actions, defines SADC Law Enforcement and Anti-Poaching strategies in the Protocol on Wildlife Conservation and Law Enforcement (1999). It emphasises harmonisation of the legal instruments regarding governing and conservation, law enforcement of wildlife laws, capacity building regarding wildlife management, establishment of transfrontier conservation areas and community-based natural resources management. Besides the Law Enforcement and Anti-Poaching Strategy, the SADC has developed a Regional Indicative Strategic Development Plan to combat poverty whilst protecting natural resources and conservation (SADC RISDP, 2001). Based on this plan, operationalisation plans have been developed, including the Food, Agriculture and Natural Resources Directorate (FANR, 2007), to define activities, and the SADC Regional Biodiversity Action Plan (SADC RBAP, 2013) to conserve a rich biodiversity.

As research shows, many strategic plans have been developed; however, the SADC (2015, p. 27) concludes that the responses to law enforcement strategies in the wildlife crises have mostly stayed uncoordinated, are hardly implemented and are often not updated. Furthermore, it is criticised that information exchange and cross-border cooperation are hardly implemented. The SADC (2015, p. 28) constitutes that the presence of police, customs, immigration and security agencies is inefficient and insufficient and that the success in wildlife crime combat is mainly achieved by professional units which are usually specialised in other crime areas, such as drug trafficking. The paper highlights that the use of outside intelligence staff might be more effective than to train the internal wildlife agency intelligence personnel. Moreover, NGOs are viewed as extraordinarily helpful in the fight against wildlife crime, as well as a view on wildlife crime which defines it as a "security issue" for increased attention (SADC, 2015, p. 29).

In terms of law enforcement, field operations are implemented which are joint operations between army, police and paramilitary parts of wildlife agencies. These operationalisations are often referred to as the green militarisation movement (e.g. Shaw et al., 2016). Increased future cooperation with international agencies, such as Interpol, is suggested, and cross-border cooperation in terms of judicial (apprehension, arrest, prosecution, conviction and sentencing) and law enforcement cooperation should be pursued (SADC, 2015, p. 29). Finally, increased manpower, as well as higher budgets, needs to be allocated for a larger law enforcement impact. In this context, army personnel has been deployed, for example, along the border between Kruger National Park and Mozambique in an attempt to improve the monitoring and controlling of the transport of rhino horn across the border, where escape is easier and punishment less severe (Shaw, 2011).

The strategies outlined by the SADC (2015) are addressed through different operations, for example, the Lusaka Agreement Task Force (LATF), the Wildlife Enforcement Network (WEN) or the Wildlife Enforcement Network for Southern Africa (WENSA). Further on, training workshops are held, and resources are allocated, whilst mission statements and visions are implemented to support African countries to combat wildlife crime who, most of the time, suffer from the poor implementation of their "good legislation" (SADC, 2015, p. 34).

The SADC (2015) emphasises that based on the legislation, sentencing guidelines should be developed appropriately, laws need to be operationalised and legislation should address all key issues in wildlife crime. International mechanisms should be domesticated on national levels. Besides that, wildlife crime must be defined as a "serious crime", which is often not the case and therefore treated with lenience and ineffectively. Furthermore, the public within the countries should be aware of the seriousness, and impact of wildlife crime and good intelligence is needed to conduct crime scene analysis and informing operations. Therefore, intelligence needs to be funded, trained and well managed in the context of inter-agency collaboration which should happen in national and regional cooperation (SADC, 2015).

Moreover—and particularly relevant for this study—wildlife crime investigators should be well-trained, and crime scenes should be treated with care and knowledge of the investigator. Often, evidence is handled unconsciously and inappropriately, so that law cases were lost due to ignorance, irresponsibility or corruption on the side of investigators and law enforcement agencies (SADC, 2015, p. 35). Henson, Malpas, and D'Udine (2016) provide insights into best practices of law enforcement in wildlife crime in sub-Saharan Africa. They emphasise that law enforcement capacities must be strengthened on national and site levels with regard to law enforcement patrols, law enforcement management and intelligence and investigations.

Law enforcement patrols, who are "at the frontline of a site's anti-poaching efforts" (Henson et al., 2016, p. xiii), need capabilities and motivation, an appropriate recruitment process, in-service training and provision of equipment, financial rewards as well as knowledge of the responsibilities and powers and legal mandate to ensure law enforcement on the micro-level of implementation.

Law enforcement management should implement activities on the base of organisational capacity. Law enforcement managers should undergo leadership training, have authority in decision-making, frontline experience and develop proactive patrol strategies. They should additionally implement effective management systems and law enforcement infrastructure, as well as standard operating procedures, staff ethics and integrity. This is of particular importance since the criminal and organised networks and their operations are resilient and resourceful (Shaw & Reitano, 2013) as well as intricate and adaptable (Ayling, 2013). Owen (2014) emphasises that this sustainability and adaptability are strongly supported by corrupt structures in law enforcement and legal systems in South Africa, as well as by the fact that the country is split in terms of what is believed to be the best response and solution to the wildlife crime crisis.

Finally, intelligence and investigations need to focus on specialising intelligence and investigation staff and capacities (Henson et al., 2016). Skills need to be developed, equipment and resources provided.

This study plays a role in developing equipment which can easily be used in crime scenes by intelligence, investigators or even other professionals who have access to the crime scene. For intelligence to be effective, reliable data gathering systems are needed and evaluated and distributed through electronic information evaluations which deal with the analysis, evaluation and report of the data collected (Henson et al., 2016, p. 43). This requires a solid budget and human resources, as well as a balance of effective tools which are low cost and simple to handle in remote areas.

As Henson et al. (2016) report, physical evidence is required to resolve wildlife crime, and robust procedures are needed for collecting, analysing and evaluating data which are admissible in court. Basic equipment is needed at crime scenes to collect and store data, and inter-agency collaboration can support prosecution proceedings.

One major problem is the "robustness of scene handling and evidence collection" by intelligence officers who are often "self-selected" and miss suitable training and/or coaching in collection, analysis and case preparation (Henson et al., 2016, p. 43). Law enforcement officers should be trained in general investigation methods, techniques of crime investigation and managing evidence, whilst being prepared with simple-to-use and affordable techniques to conduct investigations at crime scenes and to collect admissible evidence (Henson et al., 2016, p. 45). Henson et al. (2016, p. 54) criticise that there are only limited tools and "proof collection kits that ensure the chain of evidence is maintained" which are available. Only a few laboratories which "are able to extract and analyse DNA from ivory samples and which are often far away from the source countries" are accessible. These shortages are addressed in this study, as referred to in Chap. 3.

2.7 Chapter Summary

This chapter provides a brief overview on how wildlife is defined and outlines the challenges wildlife conservation faces on the African continent and within South African. In addition, wildlife crime in South Africa is described, and law enforcement with regard to the African context is critically discussed.

References

Ashley, C., & Wolmer, W. (2003). *Transforming or tinkering?: New forms of engagement between communities and the private sector in tourism and forestry in Southern Africa* (Sustainable Livelihoods in Southern Africa Programme). Sussex: University of Sussex.

Ayling, J. (2013). What sustains wildlife crime? Rhino horn trading and the resilience of criminal networks. *Journal of International Wildlife Law & Policy, 16*, 57–80.

Beirne, P., & South, N. (2007). *Issues in green criminology: Confronting harms against environments, humanity and other animals*. Devon: Willam Publishing.

Bennett, E. L. (2015a). Another inconvenient truth: The failure of enforcement systems to save charismatic species. In G. Wuerthner, E. Crist, & T. Butler (Eds.), *Protecting the wild: Parks and Wilderness* (pp. 189–193). Washington, DC: Island Press/Center for Resource Economics.

Bennett, E. L. (2015b). Legal ivory trade in a corrupt wold and its impact on African elephant populations. *Conservation Biology, 29*(1), 54–60.

Benton, T. (1998). Rights and justice on a shared planet: More rights or new relations? *Theories in Criminology, 2*(2), 149–175.
Biggs, D., Courchamp, F., Martin, R., & Possingham, H. P. (2013). Conservation. Legal trade of Africa's rhino horns. *Science, 339*, 1038–1039.
Brisman, A. (2014). Of theory and meaning in green criminology. *International Journal of Crime, Justice and Social Democracy, 3*(2), 21–34.
Brisman, A., & South, N. (2013). A green cultural criminology: An exploratory outline. *Crime Media Culture, 9*(2), 115–135.
Brisman, A., & South, N. (2014). *Green cultural criminology: Constructions of environmental harm, consumerism and resistance to ecocide*. Oxford: Routledge.
Brisman, A., South, N., & White, R. (2016). *Environmental crime and social conflict. Contemporary and emerging issues* (Green criminology series). London: Routledge.
Brockington, D., Duffy, R., & Igoe, J. (2008). *Nature unbound: Conservation, capitalism and the future of protected areas*. London: Routledge.
Büscher, B. (2013). *Transforming the frontier. "Peace parks" and the politics of neoliberal conservation in Southern Africa*. Durham: Duke University Press. Retrieved from http://library.wur.nl/WebQuery/clc/2032513
Challender, D. W. S. (2011). Asian pangolins: Increasing affluence driving hunting pressure. *TRAFFIC Bulletin, 23*, 92–93.
Challender, D. W. S., & MacMillan, D. C. (2014). Poaching is more than an enforcement problem. *Conservation Letters, 7*(5), 484–494.
CITES. (2008). *What is CITES? Convention on international trade in endangered species of wild fauna and flora*. Geneva: *CITES Secretariat*. Retrieved from www.cites.org/eng/disc/what.shtml
Convention on the International Trade of Endangered Species (CITES). (1973). *Convention on Internaitonal Trade in Endangered Species of Wild Fauna and Flora*. Retrieved from: https://www.cites.org/sites/default/files/eng/disc/CITES-Convention-EN.pdf.
Convention on the International Trade of Endangered Species (CITES). (2015). *List of contracting parties*. Retrieved from: https://www.cites.org/eng/disc/parties/gaborone.php.
Cloete, P. C., Van Der Merwe, P., & Saayman, M. (2015). *Game ranch profitability in South Africa* (2nd ed.). Pretoria: Caxton.
Courouble, M., Hursh, F., & Milliken, T. (2003). *More ivory than elephants: Domestic markets in three West African countries* (Traffic Online Report Series, No. 8, Traffic East/Southern Africa). Cambridge, UK: Traffic International.
Cousins, J. A., Sadler, J. P., & Evans, J. (2010). Exploring the role of private wildlife ranching as a conservation tool in South Africa: Stakeholder perspectives. *Ecology and Society, 13*(2), 43. Retrieved from: http://www.ecologyandsociety.org/vol13/iss2/art43/
Dalton, D. L., & Kotze, A. (2010). DNA barcoding as a tool for species identification in three forensic wildlife cases in South Africa. *Forensic Science International, 207*(1–3), 51–54.
Damm, G. (2005). Hunting in South Africa: Facts, risks and opportunities. *African Indaba, 3*, 1–14.
DRDLR. (2011). *Green paper on land reform*. Retrieved from: http://www.gov.za/sites/www.gov.za/files/land_reform_green_paper.pdf
Duncker, L. C., & Goncalves, D. (2017). *Community perceptions and attitudes regarding wildlife crime in South Africa.* http://waset.org/publications/10006465/community-perceptions-and-attitudes-regarding-wildlife-crime-in-south-africa
ECEC. (2015). *Environmental compliance and enforcement committee (ECEC) and working groups.* Retrieved from: https://www.interpol.int/Crime-areas/Environmental-crime/Committee-and-Working-Groups/Wildlife-Crime-Working-Group
Eliason, S. L. (2008). Wildlife crime: Conservation officer's perceptions of elusive poachers. *Deviant Behavior, 29*(2), 111–128.
Ferreira, S., Botha, J., & Emmett, M. (2012). Anthropogenic influences on conservation values of white rhinoceros. *PLoS ONE, 7*, 1–14.

Flynn, M., & Hall, M. (2016). The case for a victimology of nonhuman animal harms. *Contemporary Justice Review, 20*(3), 299–318.
Griffiths, M. (2017). The cultural impact of wildlife crime in South Africa. *South African Crime Quarterly, 60*, 45–50.
Guerette, R. T., & Bowers, K. J. (2009). Assessing the extent of crime displacement and diffusion of benefits: A review of situational crime prevention evaluations. *Criminology, 47*(4), 1331–1368.
Hall, M. (2017). Exploring the cultural dimensions of environmental victimization. *Palgrave Communications, 3*, 17076. Retrieved from: https://www.nature.com/articles/palcomms201776
Harvey, R. (2016). Risks and fallacies associated with promoting a legalised trade in ivory. *Politikon, 43*(2), 215–229.
Henson, D. W., Malpas, R. C., & D'Udine, F. A. C. (2016). *Wildlife law enforcement in Sub-Saharan African protected areas. A review of best practices*. Cambridge, UK: International Union for Conservation of Nature and Natural Resources.
Herbig, J. (2010). The illegal reptile trade as a form of conservation crime: A South African criminological investigation. In R. White (Ed.), *Global environmental harm. Criminological perspectives*. London: Routledge.
Hübschle, A. (2016a). Security coordination in an illegal market: the transnational trade in rhinoceros horn. *Politikon, 43*(2), 193–214.
Hübschle, A. (2016b). *A game of horns: Transnational flows of Rhino horn*. Köln: International Max Planck Research School.
Hübschle, A. (2017, September 20). South Africa: The fight against poaching must shift to empowering communities. *The Conservation*. Retrieved from: https://conservationaction.co.za/recent-news/south-africa-fight-poaching-must-shift-empowering-communities/
Institute for Security Studies. (2017, September 21). *Horns, guns and drugs: The real cost of wildlife crime*. Retrieved from: https://issafrica.org/about-us/press-releases/horns-guns-and-drugs-the-real-cost-of-wildlife-crime
Jones, B., & Weaver, C. (2008). CBNRM in Namibia: growth, trends, lessons and constraints. In evolution and innovation in wildlife conservation in southern Africa. In H. Suich, B. Child, & A. Spenceley (Eds.), *Evolution and innovation in wildlife conservation: Parks and game ranches to transfrontier conservation areas* (pp. 223–242). London, UK: Earthscan.
Kepe, T., Wynberg, R., & Ellis, W. (2005). Land reform and biodiversity conservation in South Africa: complementary or in conflict? *International Journal of Biodiversity Science and Management, 1*, 3–16.
Lambrechts, D., & Goga, K. (2016). Money and marginalisation: the lost war against Abalone poaching in South Africa. *Politikon, 43*(2), 231–249.
Lemieuy, A. M., & Clarke, R. V. (2009). The international ban on ivory sales and its effects on elephant poaching in Africa. *British Journal of Criminology, 49*, 451–471.
Lindsey, P. A., & Taylor, W. A. (2012). *A study on the dehorning of African rhinoceroses as a tool to reduce the risk of poaching*. Pretoria: Department of Environmental Affairs.
Lindsey, P. A., Balme, G., Becker, M., Begg, C., Bento, C., Bocchino, C., et al. (2013). The bushmeat trade in African savannas: Impacts, drivers, and possible solutions. *BiologicalConservation, 160*, 80–96.
Lynch, M. J., & Stretesky, P. B. (2014). *Exploring green criminology: Toward a green criminology revolution*. Farnham: Ashgate.
Martin, R. B. (2012). *A legal trade in rhino horn: Hobson's choice*. Johannesburg, South Africa: Rhino Survival Trust.
Michel, A. L., Bengis, R. G., Hofmeyr, M., de Klerk, L. M., Cross, P. C., Jolles, A. E., et al. 463 (2006). Wildlife tuberculosis in South African conservation areas: Implications and challenges. 464. *Veterinary Microbiology, 112*(2–4), 91–100.
Moreto, W. D. (2016). Occupational stress among law enforcement rangers: Insights from Uganda. *Oryx, 50*(4), 646–654.

Newmark, W. D., & Hough, J. L. (2000). Conserving wildlife in Africa: Integrating conservation and development projects and beyond: Because multiple factors hinder integrated conservation and development projects in Africa from achieving their objectives, alternative and complementary approaches for promoting wildlife conservation must be actively explored. *BioScience, 50*(7), 585–592.

Nurse, A. (2015). *Policing wildlife: Perspectives on the enforcement of wildlife legislation*. London: Palgrave Macmillan.

Nurse, A. (2017). Green criminology: Shining a critical lens on environmental harm. *Palgrave Communications, 3*(10), 1–4.

Owen, R. (2014, January 17). *Ground for weeds to grow: Why international crime syndicates favour SA*. Retrieved from: http://www.financialmail.co.za/features/2014/01/16/why-international-crime-syndicates-favour-sa

Ramutsindela, M. (2016). Wildlife crime and state security in South(ern) Africa: An overview of developments. *Politikon, 43*(2), 159–171.

Reilly, B. K., Sutherland, E. A., & Harley, V. (2003). The nature and extent of wildlife ranching in Gauteng province, South Africa. *South African Journal of Wildlife Research, 32*(2), 141–144.

SA Government. (1996). *Green paper transforming public service delivery*. Department of Public Service and Administration. Retrieved from: https://www.gov.za/sites/default/files/pubservice_0.pdf

SABC. (2018, March 3). *Wildlife crime a burden for economic development and opportunities*. Retrieved from: http://www.sabcnews.com/sabcnews/wildlife-crime-burden-economic-development-opportunities/

Shaw, J. (2011). *Poaching crisis in South Africa: The South African situation*. Save the Rhino International. Retrieved from: https://www.savetherhino.org/rhino_info/thorny_issues/poaching_crisis_in_south_africa

Shaw, M., & Reitano, T. (2013). *The evolution of organised crime in Africa: Towards a new response* (Institute for Security Studies Paper, 244). Pretoria: Institute for Security Studies. Retrieved from: https://issafrica.org/research/papers/the-evolution-of-organised-crime-in-africa-towards-a-new-response

Shaw, A., Miller, K.K. & Wescott, G.C. (2016). Wildlife gardening and connectedness to nature: engaging the unengaged, Environmental Vlaues, *22*(4), 483–502.

Snijders, D. (2012). Wild property and its boundaries—on wildlife policy and rural consequences in South Africa. *The Journal of Peasant Studies, 39*(2), 503–520.

Snijders, D. (2015). *Shifting species in South Africa. Wildlife policy, rural consequences* (Doctoral dissertation). University of Amsterdam. Retrieved from: http://www.rhinoresourcecenter.com/pdf_files/142/1422583600.pdf

South African Development Community. (1999). Protocol on wildlife conservation and law enforcement. Retrieved from: http://www.sadc.int/files/4813/7042/6186/Wildlife_Conservation.pdf.

South African Development Community (SADC) Regional Indicative Strategic Development (RISDP). (2001). *Southern African Development Community Regional Indicative Strategic Development Plan*. Retrieved from: http://www.sadc.int/files/5713/5292/8372/Regional_Indicative_Strategic_Development_Plan.pdf.

South African Development Community. (2015). *Law enforcement and anti-poaching strategy*. Retrieved from: http://www.gaborone.diplo.de/contentblob/4715602/Daten/6225475/SADC_LEAP_FINAL.pdf

South African Development Community (SADC) Food, Agricultural and Natural Resources Directorate FANR. (2007). *Food agriculture and natural resources*. Retrieved from: http://www.sadc.int/sadc-secretariat/directorates/office-deputy-executive-secretary-regional-integration/food-agriculture-natural-resources/

South African Development Community (SADC) Regional Biodiversity Action Plan. (2013). *Overview of the SADC regional biodiversity strategy & SADC regional biodiversity action plan*. Southern Africa NBSAP Workshop, 14–20 March 2011, Kasane, Botswana. Retrieved from: https://www.cbd.int/doc/nbsap/nbsapcbw-safr-02/SADC%20Regional%20BSAP.pdf

South, N. (2010). The ecocidal tendencies of late modernity: Transnational crime, social exclusions, victims and rights. In R. White (Ed.), *Global environmental harm: Criminological perspective* (pp. 228–247). Devon: William Publishing.

South, N., & Wyatt, T. (2011). Comparing illicit trades in wildlife and drugs: an exploratory study. *Deviant Behaviour, 32*(6), 538–361.

Stiles, D. (2004). The ivory trade and elephant conservation. *Environmental Conservation, 31*, 309–321.

Tapela, B. N., & Omara-Ojungu, P. H. (1999). Towards bridging the gap between wildlife conservation and rural development in post-apartheid South Africa: The case of the Makulele community and the Kruger National Park. *South African Geographical Journal, 81*(3), 148–155.

Taylor, A., Lindsey, P., & Davies-Mostert, H. (2016). *An assessment of the economic, social and conservation value of the wildlife ranching industry and its potential to support the green economy in South Africa. Green Economy Research Report*. Johannesburg: The Endangered Wildlife Trust. Retrieved from: http://www.the-eis.com/data/literature/Taylor%20et%20al%20%202016%20An%20assessment%20of%20the%20economic%20social%20and%20conservation%20value%20of%20the%20wildlife%20ranching%20industry%20and%20its%20potential%20to%20support%20the%20green%20e.pdf

The National Agricultural Marketing Council. (2006). *Report on the investigation to identify problems for sustainable growth and development in South African wildlife ranching*. Pretoria: NAMC.

United Nations. (2008). *United Nations convention on transnational organized crime*. Retrieved from: http://www.uncjin.org/Documents/Conventions/dcatoc/final_documents_2/convention_eng.pdf

van Uhm, D. P. (2016). *The illegal wildlife trade: Inside the world of poachers, smugglers ad traders*. Rotterdam: Springer.

van Uhm, D. P. (2018). The social construction of the value of wildlife: A green cultural criminological perspective. *Theoretical Criminology, 22*(3), 384–401.

von Essen, E., & Allen, M. (2017). Interspecies violence and crimes of dissent: Communication ethics and legitimacy in message crimes involving wildlife. *Critical Criminology, 25*(2), 261–274.

Warchol, G. (2004). The transnational illegal wildlife trade. *Criminal Justice Studies, 17*(1), 57–73.

Warchol, G., & Johnson, B. (2011). Wildlife crime in the game reserves in South Africa: A research note. *International Journal of Comparative and Applied Criminal Justice, 33*(1), 143–154.

Wittemyer, G., Northrup, J. M., Blanc, J., Douglas-Hamilton, I., Omondi, P., & Burnham, K. P. (2014). Illegal killing for ivory drives global decline in African elephants. *Proceedings of the National Academy of Sciences, 111*, 13117–13121.

Wong, R. (2016). The organization of the illegal tiger parts trade in China. *British Journal of Criminology, 56*(5), 995–1013.

Wyatt, T. (2009). Exploring the organization of Russia far East's illegal wildlife trade: Two case studies of the illegal fur and illegal falcon trades. *Global Crime, 10*(1–2), 144–154.

Chapter 3
Forensic Trace Recovery in Green Criminology

3.1 Chapter Preview

This theoretical chapter outlines firstly the general issues associated with green criminology and forensic trace recovery and secondly emphasises the seizure and maximisation of forensic potential in terms of formal identification. It addresses the issue of extrinsic and intrinsic evidence. The value of the worldwide crime forensics will be outlined. The chapter closes with a chapter summary.

3.2 Introducing Forensic Trace Recovery in Green Criminology

In forensic trace recovery in green criminology, the range of forensic methods to tackle crime has increased, and the techniques have grown to become more sophisticated (FWG, 2014). In their book *Wildlife Forensics: Methods and Applications*, Huffman and Wallace (2012) present an accessible and practical approach to wildlife forensics. The editors show case studies in different areas of wildlife forensics and cover experiences in the range from lab analytics to courtroom proceedings. Further, the editors refer to developing DNA profiling systems for game species and microscopic hair characterisation (Huffman & Wallace, 2012). The Forensic Working Group (FWG, 2014) describes extensively the scenes of crime examinations, including the taking of fingerprints, fibres, hair and fur, as well as footwear, tyre and instrument marks and other traces. Moore and Kornfield (2012), who describe best practices in wildlife forensics, argue for the need for appropriate standards in wildlife forensics, whilst Espinoza, Espinoza, Trail, and Baker (2012) propose that enhancing wildlife protection needs to happen through integrating forensic science and the law, recreating endangered species and highlighting the

C.-H. Mayer, *Combating Wildlife Crime in South Africa*, SpringerBriefs in Criminology, https://doi.org/10.1007/978-3-030-05891-3_3

limits of sciences. Linacre and Tobe (2013) specialise in DNA testing for wildlife crime investigation and emphasise as well the importance of the role of forensic science in wildlife crime investigation in cooperation with a specific legislation covering wildlife crime.

Forensic science is only employable when the legislation is breached on national and international levels (Linacre & Tobe, 2013). Thereby, the Convention on International Trade in Endangered Species of Wild Fauna and Flora (CITES)—which was founded in 1973—has 175 member countries which have signed the convention. On a national level, member countries enact laws to implement and enforce CITES, whilst they, at the same time, enact laws to protect wildlife within the country (Linacre & Tobe, 2013). Hall (2017), however, points out that green criminology has still got a long way to go since methodologies, research strategies and values in green criminology are lacking depth and need to be studied further to finally support law enactment on local, regional and global levels. Van Uhm (2018) also argues that wildlife crime always needs to be viewed and understood in socio-cultural and historical perspectives, since wildlife trade and the value of wildlife have historically been constructed around "exotic animals" and social elities, whilst contemporarily wildlife trade is attractive for a broader range of individuals all over the world and often traded with regard to functional, symbolic and social purposes. Van Uhm (2018) therefore argues for a culture-sensitive approach to green criminology and the integration of cultural criminological constructs and green criminology.

In the South African context, law enactment, conservation issues, green criminology and its combat are strongly involved in socio-political and historical issues of Apartheid, since conservation and wildlife issues are related to the ranches and the tourism industry which are predominantly run by one population group in South Africa, namely the Whites (Smith & Humphreys, 2016). This is why Smith and Humphreys (2016) emphasise that wildlife crime and combat need to be viewed and placed into context with regard to sociocultural and historical issues, security and conservation themes and can not be discussed independently of this very specific cultural context.

3.3 Forensic Trace Recovery and Law Enforcement

Internationally, scientists wonder why law enforcement agencies are failing to tackle wildlife crime to conserve decreasing animal species. Bennett (2015, p. 189) points out that law enforcement agencies are not equipped to deal with "sophisticated organized criminal syndicates", since they were not established to tackle such crime. Law enforcement suffers from low governance, missing resources, low capacity building and limited personal, technological and financial capacities. Bennett (2015) also emphasises that highly trained personnel and technology are needed to cope with the demand and functioning networks of committed governments and NGOs. However, the trained personnel and the technology needed to trace the crime and the criminals, their networks and organisations are not always available (see Sect. 2.4). Henson et al. (2016, p. 54) criticise that there are only limited forensic tools and evaluation laboratories, and Ogden, Dawnay, and McEwing (2009) emphasise that wildlife DNA forensics are urgently needed for developing and using investigative tools to ensure successful wildlife law enforcement and protection of endangered species. Thereby, DNA forensics aim at identifying the species traded and their origins and traders whilst applying quality assurance standards.

Research on illegal trade in African elephant ivory with DNA forensics has pointed out that international criminal activity and trade of wildlife is extremely expensive and difficult to track. This being due to the fact that for a long time, forensic investigations have:

> typically been unable to determine the geographic origins of poached ivory because their information generally begins at the point of shipping, yet ivory may or may not be exported from the same country in which it was poached. (Wasser et al., 2008, p. 1070)

The authors, however, have previously shown that forensic methods to examine the geographic origin(s) of seized ivory can support the assessment of criminal networks regarding wildlife crime (Wasser et al., 2004, 2007) and to determine where the seized ivory originated. Wasser et al. (2008) found through DNA analysis that criminal syndicates used a decentralised plan of ivory gathering. Findings showed that criminal networks make specific decisions on which areas to exploit on a large scale before moving to the next area to exploit strategically. Findings also emphasised that country-crossing approaches are used strategically to diffuse the network structure, and researchers highlighted that "these patterns would have been really impossible to uncover without genetic forensic tools" (Wasser et al., 2008, p. 1070).

3.4 Forensic Trace Recovery and Gelatine Lifting

The application of forensic investigation tools and techniques were primarily used shortly after DNA analysis was applied to human forensic investigations (Gill, Jeffreys, & Werrett, 1985; Huffman & Wallace, 2012). Sir Alec Jeffreys realised, when studying a gene in grey seals, that methods could be applied to humans and could be used to link family groups (Linacre & Tobe, 2013). Burke and Bruford (1987) emphasised that soon after similar processes were applied to nonhuman samples. This later on became the process of DNA fingerprinting (Jeffreys, Wilson, & Thein, 1985). Further on, DNA analysis was used to investigate cases of illegal trade (Baker & Palumbi, 1994) and for purposes of investigating poaching (Sweijd et al., 1998). Contemporary, DNA analysis is used to investigate wildlife crime, to identify animal remains and to ascertain the circumstances of death of wild species and other legal proceedings and activities concerning wildlife (crime) (Cooper & Cooper, 2013). Additionally, the editors point out that the most important aspect in wildlife crime combat is to keep up to date and keep an open mind to new developments and evolving techniques of investigation and scientific skills (Cooper & Cooper, 2013). According to Ogden et al. (2009), a wide range of molecular identification methods are used nowadays. Whilst these methods create many opportunities for tracing wildlife crime, they also create various challenges.

Gelatine lifters support the evidence collection of physical (e.g. fingerprints, footprints, shoeprints), biological (e.g. feathers, skin, blood) or botanical (e.g. pollen, leaves, root traces) evidence markers at the wildlife crime scene and/or on the traded material (Hamilton & Erhart, 2012, p. 69). DNA fingerprint tracking has advanced as an important tool and technique that analyses sequences of DNA known as microsatellites (Wasser, Clark, & Laurie, 2009). The use of gelatine lifters has been described previously, and clear instructions on how to use gelatine lifters in the field have been provided (NPIA, 2007). Smith and Bond (2015) further on provide insight on how gelatine lifters are used in crime scene investigation and how the evidence might be used in law enforcement and in the context of criminal justice.

Most commonly in wildlife DNA forensics, genetic sample analysis is used to identify the species of an evidence sample (Ogden et al., 2009). However, the exploration of genetic markers is not only a vivid research field but also the identification of profiling of trace recovery at the crime scene and on the traded products, such as fingerprints, footprints, shoeprints, etc., as assumed in this study.

Although the method of lifting marks with gelatine lifters has been used for many years, it was only until commercial gelatine lifters were developed that trace recovery has become more efficient and applicable (Wiesner, Tsach, Belser, & Shor, 2011). Gelatine lifters have been studied with regard to lifting marks in blood (Theeuwen et al., 1998; Velders, 1996) and fingerprints (Bleay, Bandey, Black, & Sears, 2011). However, research has—as described in Hammell, Deacon, and Farrugia (2014)—hardly been tested with regard to lifting soil-based marks after chemical treatment. The authors emphasise in reference to gelatine lifting that the lifted mark is a mirror image of the original mark and that the mark on the lifter depends rather on the substrate used than on the chemical enhancement technique applied.

Trace evidence is "best described as any small piece of evidence" that has to be collected by forensic investigators (Claridge, 2016). Extrinsic trace evidence can include the skin, bloodstains, soil, glass, grass, fibres and hair, and these elements can be classified as micro scene elements. Hair and fibre evidence is normally used as associative evidence and has a specific intrinsic investigative value which might demonstrate that there may be an association between, for example, a suspect and a crime scene or a suspect and a victim or that there is no association (Shaler, 2011). Furthermore, hair evidence, with regard to the basic structure of hair, from a DNA perspective, can provide potential forensic value.

This study focuses on the seizure and maximisation of forensic potential in terms of formal identification through fingerprints and DNA. It further explores indications of provenance through extrinsic trace materials which are adhered to the ivory and packaging materials whilst also focusing on the more intrinsic evidence available through physical sampling of the ivory itself, using techniques, such as isotope analysis. Trace evidence using gelatine lifters is collected, following the research methodology explained in Chap. 4.

3.5 Chapter Summary

This chapter provides insights into the importance of techniques of forensic trace recovery to combat international wildlife crime and horn and ivory trade. It provides the reader with an argument as to why forensic trace recovery methods need to be researched and how they can contribute to defining criminal networks as well as products illegally traded. Finally, forensic trace recovery within the field of green criminology is discussed and the value of green criminology for worldwide wildlife crime forensics emphasised.

References

Baker, C. S., & Palumbi, S. R. (1994). Which whales are hunted? A molecular genetic approach to monitoring whaling. *Science, 265*, 1538–1539.

Bennett, E. L. (2015). Another inconvenient truth: the failure of enforcement systems to save chrismatic species. In G. Wuerthner, E. Crist, & T. Butler (Eds.), *Protecting the wild: Parks and Wilderness* (pp. 189–193). Washington, DC: Island Press/Center's for Resource Economics.

Bleay, S. M., Bandey, H. L., Black, M., & Sears, V. G. (2011). The gelatin lifting process: An evaluation of its effectiveness in the recovery of latent fingerprints. *Journal of Forensic Identification, 61*(6), 581–606.

Burke, T., & Bruford, M. W. (1987). DNA fingerprinting in birds. *Nature, 327*, 149–152.

Claridge, J. (2016, December 5). *Understanding trace evidence.* Retrieved from: http://www.exploreforensics.co.uk/understanding-trace-evidence.html

Cooper, J. E., & Cooper, M. E. (Eds.). (2013). *Wildlife forensic investigation—principles and practice*. Boca Raton: CRC Press.

Espinoza, E. O., Espinoza, J. L., Trail, P. W., & Baker, B. W. (2012). The future of wildlife forensic science. In J. E. Huffman & J. R. Wallace (Eds.), *Wildlife forensics methods and applications* (pp. 343–356). Oxford: Wiley-Blackwell.

FWG Forensic Working Group. (2014). *Wildlife Crime. A guide to the use of forensic and specialist techniques in the investigation of wildlife crime*. London: Crown. Retrieved from: https://www.tracenetwork.org/wp-content/uploads/2012/08/Wildlife-Crime-use-of-forensics-FWG-April-2014.pdf

Gill, P., Jeffreys, A. J., & Werrett, D. J. (1985). Forensic applications of DNA "fingerprints". *Nature, 218*, 577–579.

Hall, M. (2017). Doing "green criminology": Methodologies, research strategies and values (or lack thereof?). In M. Hall, T. Wyatt, N. South, A. Nurse, G. Potter, & J. Maher (Eds.), *Greening criminology in the 21st century. Centemporary debates and future directions in the study of environmental harm* (pp. 35–62). London: Taylor & Francis.

Hamilton, M. D., & Erhart, E. M. (2012). Forensic evidence collection and cultural motives for animal harvesting. In J. E. Huffman & J. R. Wallace (Eds.), *Wildlife forensics. Methods and applications* (pp. 65–80). Oxford: Wiley-Blackwell.

Hammell, L., Deacon, P., & Farrugia, K. J. (2014). Chemical enhancement of soil-based marks on nonporous surfaces followed by gelatin lifting. *Journal of Forensic Identification, 64*(6), 583–608.

Henson, D. W., Malpas, R. C., & D'Udine, F. A. C. (2016). *Wildlife law enforcement in Sub-Saharan African protected areas. A review of best practices*. Cambridge, UK: International Union for Conservation of Nature and Natural Resources.

Huffman, J. E., & Wallace, J. R. (2012). *Wildlife forensics. Methods and applications*. Oxford: Wiley-Blackwell.
Jeffreys, A. J., Wilson, V., & Thein, S. L. (1985). Individual-specific fingerprints of human DNA. *Nature, 316*, 76–79.
Linacre, A. T., & Tobe, S. S. (2013). *DNA analysis. Applications in forensic science*. Chichester, West Sussex: Wiley-Blackwell.
Moore, M. K., & Kornfield, I. L. (2012). Best practices in wildlife forensic DNA. In J. E. Huffman & J. R. Wallace (Eds.), *Wildlife forensics. Methods and applications* (pp. 201–231). Oxford: Wiley-Blackwell.
NPIA. (2007). *Footwear marks recovery manual*. National Policing Improvement Agency. Retrieved from: http://library.college.police.uk/docs/appref/NPIA-(2007)-Footwear-Marks-Recovery-Manual.pdf
Ogden, R., Dawnay, N., & McEwing, R. (2009). Wildlife DNA forensics—bridging the gap between conservation genetics and law enforcement. *Endangered Species Research, 9*, 179–195.
Shaler, R. C. (2011). *Crime scene forensics: A scientific method approach*. Boca Raton: CRC Press.
Smith, L., & Bond, J. (2015). *Criminal justice and forensic science. A multidisciplinary introduction*. London: Palgrave.
Smith, M. L. R., & Humphreys, J. (2016). The poaching paradox: Why South Africa's "Rhino Wars" shina a harsh sportlight on security and conservation. In A. Brisman, N. South, & R. White (Eds.), *Environmental crime and social conflict. Contemporary and emerging issues* (Green Criminology Series) (pp. 197–220). London: Routledge.
Sweijd, N. A., Bowie, E. C. K., Lopata, A. L., Marinaki, A. M., Harley, E. H., & Cook, P. A. (1998). A PCR technique for forensic, species-level identification of abalone tissue. *Journal of Shellfish Research, 17*, 889–895.
Theeuwen, A. B. E., van Barneveld, S., Drok, J. W., Keereweer, I., Limborgh, J. C. M., Naber, W. M., et al. (1998). Enhancement of Footwear Impressions in Blood. *Forensic Science International, 95*(2), 133–151.
van Uhm, D. P. (2018). The social construction of the value of wildlife: A green cultural criminological perspective. *Theoretical Criminology, 22*(3), 384–401.
Velders, M. J. M. (1996). *Fluorescing traces in blood on white gelatin lifters with Hungarian red*. Presented at the 81st Educational Conference of the International Association of Identification, Greensboro, NC.
Wasser, S. K., Clark, B., & Laurie, C. (2009). The ivory trail. *Conservation, 301*(1), 68–76.
Wasser, S. K., Clark, W. J., Drori, O., Kisamo, E. S., Mailand, C., Mutayoba, B., et al. (2008). Combating the illegal trade in African elephant ivory with DNA forensics. *Conservation Biology, 22*(4), 1065–1071.
Wasser, S. K., Mailand, C., Booth, R., Mutayoba, B., Kisamo, E., Clark, B., et al. (2007). Using ivory to track the origin of the largest ivory seizure since the 1989 trade ban. *Proceedings of the National Academy of Sciences of the United States of America, 104*, 4228–4233.
Wasser, S. K., Shedlock, A. M., Comstock, K., Ostrander, E. A., Mutayoba, B., & Stephens, M. (2004). Assigning elephant DNA to geographic region of origin: applications to the ivory trade. *Proceedings of the National Academy of Sciences of the United States of America, 101*, 14847–14852.
Wiesner, S., Tsach, T., Belser, C., & Shor, Y. (2011). A comparative research of two lifting methods: Electrostatic lifter and gelantin lifter. *Journal of Forensic Sciences, 56*(1), 58–62.

Chapter 4
Research Methodology

4.1 Chapter Preview

In this chapter, the research design and methodology is described, including the methodological paradigm and research approaches. Data collection and data evaluation processes, as well as the analysis, interpretation and evaluation procedures, are presented. Finally, ethical aspects are considered and methodological limitations are emphasised. The chapter closes with a chapter summary.

4.2 Anchoring the Research Methodology

Green criminology, as a fast expanding field, considers growing theoretical and methodological approaches. It needs to engage in discourses on rich and in-depth interdisciplinary theories and methodologies which help to establish the field of green criminology and its acceptance within the broader context of criminology (Sollund & Brisman, 2017). This study contributes to the research base of green criminology in the context of wildlife crime by presenting a case study approach within a culture-specific natural experiment setting.

This study is defined as a preliminary experimental case study, following an experimental research design to account for the evidential value of the traces recovered through the use of gelatine lifters in a defined area in South Africa. It thereby takes the environmental impact of the South African context (pollen, dust, heat, etc.) into account.

The case study focuses on investigating a single instance of the phenomenon of interest—which is defined as the recovery of traces from a defined natural setting on the gelatine lifters described. It follows a qualitative research paradigm (Yin, 2009), thereby assuming that reality is constructed. This construction of reality is intertwined with a context-specific approach (Patton, 2002), taking the South

C.-H. Mayer, *Combating Wildlife Crime in South Africa*, SpringerBriefs in Criminology, https://doi.org/10.1007/978-3-030-05891-3_4

African context into account. Additionally, it is asserted that real events can be observed empirically and evaluated. They can be explained through logical analysis and interpretation. Further, using micro-level experimentation will eliminate the complexity of the external world (Kaboub, 2008).

The research approach used is applied outside of a controlled setting and therefore can be classified as a "natural experiment" (Babbie & Mouton, 2007, p. 224). Conducting a natural experiment is based on a systematic conduct of sample definition, data collection as well as analysis and evaluation (Collins & Hussey, 2003). In this natural experiment, a "field setting" (Collins & Hussey, 2003, p. 64) is used.

4.3 Data Collection

In the following section, the data collection is described with regard to the field setting and sampling of data collection.

4.3.1 The Setting of Research

Data was gathered within the South African context, in the North West Province, close to the border of the Gauteng Province.

The gelatine lifters used were shipped from England, UK, to the researcher in South Africa. The researcher collected data by using gelatine lifters in selected contexts, such as indoor rooms and outdoor places, in shady and sunny areas (up to 32 °C). After the data was collected, the lifters were openly packed (without the plastic cover being placed back on the gel) into cardboard boxes. The alternative—which places the clear, previously removed, plastic cover back on the gel—was not used.

The setting of research was chosen to test the functionality and performance of gelatine lifters under the various context-specific conditions (e.g. dust, heat) and to test the usability and performance of gelatine lifters with regard to packaging and shipping across long distances.

4.3.2 Samples and Sampling

Samples including trace material with finger and footwear marks were taken by using gelatine lifters. The marks were placed on the surfaces in a random form and then recovered using the gelatine lifters. Besides the prints, other trace materials, such as pollen and dust, were collected as a side effect. All samples were taken in the same farm area in November 2016, which is late spring in South Africa with temperatures ranging from 22 to 34 °C in this area.

4.3.2.1 Description of Gelatine Lifters

The gelatine lifters that were used were scenesafe gelatine lifters.[1] The gelatine lifters were produced in the Netherlands, shipped to England and then shipped to South Africa.

The company BVDA (2012) describes the lifters as follows: The carrier (layer 1) holds the second layer of gelatine. The gelatine is kept in a flexible format, and both of the layers are covered by a protective acetate cover sheet (Hammell, Deacon, & Farrugia, 2014). The cover sheet is made out of a:

> clear polyester film which is removed prior to lifting and may be replaced once the lift is completed. (Hammell et al., 2014, p. 585)

Gelatine lifters do not create air bubbles between the lifters and the surface which provides them with advantages over adhesive lifters. Furthermore, gelatine lifters have "high light absorption properties" (Hammell et al., 2014, p. 585). This enables them to photograph faint impressions. Safranin-treated marks lifted with white gelatine lifters can be seen under fluorescent light.

The following process of using gelatine lifters was followed (as in Milne, 2013):

- Gelatine lifters were put onto potential finger-, foot- and shoeprints for a few minutes to gel lift the prints.
- The gelatine lifters were carefully lifted from the potential print, packed and stored for airmail in boxes without the gelatine lifters being covered.

The best storage method for gelatine lifters is to keep the lift uncovered in a breathable and non-shedding box (Bandey, 2008). This procedure was followed, and the (uncovered) lifters were sent in single boxes to the UK, where they were analysed as soon as possible.

4.3.2.2 Sampling Procedure

The sampling followed the described process: Selected sampling places were chosen on which finger-, shoe- and footprints were left. These places included areas within a farmhouse and outside on the farmland. The sampling criteria of collection were:

- Sample collection in a setting (70 km from Pretoria) which is similar to areas in South Africa where wild animals roam (natural traces, temperatures)
- Various sample collection places—differing in terms of indoor and outdoor areas (five places each with different surface materials, temperatures and environmental influences)

[1] Evidence recovery systems. BVDA Gellifters. Fingerprint Lifters Black. Size: 13 × 18 cm, 10 sheets. Art.no.: B20614/B – 1100W Batch no: 2015164, Manufactured: 10/2016. Best before: 10/2017. Tel: +44(0)1621786654, Email: sales@scenesafe.co.uk. Website: www.scenesafe.co.uk. Manufactured by: BVDA International, BV in the Netherlands.

First specific locations were chosen; then the finger-, foot- and shoemarks were left on the chosen places. Thereafter, gelatine lifters were used to lift the prints from the materials. It was assumed that—whilst lifting the prints—other trace materials from indoor and outdoor areas would be lifted for evaluation purposes. Dust and pollen, for example, which occur in the natural environment were supposed to be found on the lifters together with the print material.

4.3.2.3 Description of Indoor Area

Within the farmhouse, different surface materials were chosen for lifting purposes: tiles (one cold and shady place (sample 1), one sunny and warm place (sample 3)), a wooden table (cool place, sample 2), a metal lamp (cool place, sample 9), and a wooden cupboard (sample 10).

The places chosen in the indoor area were moderate (in terms of temperature). The temperature measured with a thermometer was 20 °C. The temperature of the material differed according to the material chosen, e.g. checked by hand, the temperature on the metal lamp felt colder than the temperature on the wooden cupboard; the tiles in the sun felt warmer than the tiles in the shady area.

Various test areas were chosen to test the gels' performances on different materials and under various conditions. These different test environments provide insight into the performance of the gel under these different conditions (Figs. 4.1 and 4.2).

4.3.2.4 Description of Outdoor Area

On the farm, the chosen outdoor areas were the following: Sample 4 (fingerprints) was collected on brick stones in an outdoor, savanna-like farm area. Sample 5 (shoeprint) was collected on a wooden bench near a fireplace; sample 6 (fingerprint) was collected on a plastic bin, placed not far from the fireplace. In all these places chosen, the temperatures were moderate, around 20–25 °C.

Samples 7 and 8 were taken in very dry, hot and sunny places, with temperatures up to 32 °C. Sample 7 collected a footprint on a stone area in a sunny and hot place at midday. Sample 8 collected fingerprints on a magazine paper which was placed on a table in an outdoor area in the midday sun (Table 4.1; Fig. 4.3).

4.3.2.5 Shipping of Samples from South Africa to England

For analysis, the samples were shipped to Portsmouth in England, UK. After the collection of prints on the sample gelatine lifters, the samples were packaged in boxes (uncovered) and fixed with sellotape. For each sample a single cardboard box was used. Ten boxes were then shipped (via air mail) abroad for laboratory analysis.

Fig. 4.1 Farmland area in the North West Province. (All photographs in this chapter have been taken by the author)

4.4 Data Analysis, Interpretation and Presentation

The analysis of the traces collected on the gelatine lifters can be described as a multistep process. The gelatine lifters were analysed and evaluated in the following way:

1. After lifting the traces and shipping, the gel lifter was scanned in the laboratory to determine the location of any significant marks or interaction points. The presence of any traces were graded according to their evidential value.
2. At the interaction points, where there is evidence of contact, the marks developed are examined for touch DNA and profiled using current DNA profiling techniques. These profiling techniques included the following steps: The samples were removed from the boxes and placed on a GLScan system. Each gel lift was scanned using the BVDA GLScan system, designed specifically for black gelatine lifters. The system allows visualisation of the traces on the gelatine lifts and shows the contact surface and any marks to be observed, if they are present.
3. Sections of the gelatine lifters underwent microscopy to review the presence of dust and pollens. The amount and nature of the pollens observed was recorded (although not presented in this study).
4. All outcomes were statistically analysed and evaluated regarding their prevalence and value (statistics are not presented here).

Fig. 4.2 Vegetation on farmland during sample collection

In this study, the grading was a simple matrix with the purpose of evaluating the quality of the gelatine after long-distance transition, based on the clarity of the image. The analysis was based on the following predefined criteria:

1. Integrity of the image—good; good but with distortions; no image of donor surface.
2. Presence of any marks—yes and good quality, yes but poor quality, no marks were present. Here, cross-reference to where the marks were lifted from is taken into account with regard to the likelihood of it bearing a mark. The fingermark visualisation manual (Center for Applied Science and Technology, CAST, 2014) was used, particularly refering to the surface (the quality is defined relating to the surface material—non-porous, smooth, rough, porous surfaces—and the constituents on the mark and their permeating into the surface).

Table 4.1 Date and location of samples

Sample no.	Date	Location	Sample
1	19 November 2016	Farmland area	Footprint on floor (tiles), indoor
2	20 November 2016	Farmland area	Fingerprint on wood, indoor
3	19 November 2016	Farmland area	Footprint on floor (tiles), indoor
4	20 November 2016	Farmland area	Fingerprint on stone (outdoor area)
5	19 November 2016	Farmland area	Shoeprint on woodbench (outdoor area)
6	20 November 2016	Farmland area	Handprint on plastic bin (outdoor area)
7	19 November 2016	Farmland area	Footprint on stone area—farmland, outdoor area, sunny and hot area
8	20 November 2016	Farmland area	Fingerprint on magazine paper, outdoor area, sunny and hot area
9	20 November 2016	Rustig farm	Fingerprint on metal lamp, inside area, sunny
10	19 November 2016	Farmland area	Fingerprint on wood cupboard, vertical, indoor area, cool place

Source: Author's own construction

Fig. 4.3 Place on farm close to where outdoor samples were collected

3. Indications on survivability from the pilot, taking the question into account if the remote recovery and dissemination of the gels are achievable.

The findings are interpreted from an experimental research design and qualitative research paradigm (Chap. 5).

4.5 Ethical Considerations and Methodological Limitations

This research follows the usual ethical considerations. The researcher followed the appropriate guidelines, including compliance with the South African law—holding a South African research visa at the time the research was conducted, as well as not having any conflicts of interest in the outcome of the study. Since no human beings or animals were involved in this research, ethical considerations with regard to confidentiality, non-discrimination, participant consent or social responsibility were not relevant.

However, the researcher follows an ethical approach by striving for high research standards and transparent and honest reporting of research methodology and findings, sharing research data with the research community and complying with the law and standards of the university and country the research study is based at (Portsmouth University, England), as well as with the country in which the study was conducted (South Africa).

As any research, this study comes with limitations. Firstly, this study is conducted in a natural setting and does not control for any variables influencing the data set. It does not measure external influences in an exact way (e.g. temperature on surface material) and does not compare traces lifted by controlling and comparing external influences, such as humidity or temperature. The study is limited by the fact that gel lifters were mailed to England in boxes in which the gel lifters were uncovered and breathable. The study, however, did not compare samples mailed covered/uncovered and therefore does not provide any information on the impact of the covering/uncovering of traces on the gel lifters.

Based on the limitations, this study is classified as a preliminary experimental case study.

4.6 Chapter Summary

This chapter presented the research methodology, embedding the research study briefly in the research design, paradigm and approach and emphasising its exploratory experimental case study character. The data collection process, the analysis and evaluation procedures are described. It thereby provides the basis for transparency of research and comprehensibility of the findings.

References

Babbie, E., & Mouton, J. (2007). *The practice of social research*. Oxford: Oxford University Press.

Bandey, H. L. (2008). *Special edition: Footwear mark recovery* (Fingerprint and footwear forensics newsletter, 24(08)). St. Alban: H.O.S.D.B. Publications.

BVDA. (2012). *Gellifters: Lift your evidence to the highest level.* Retrieved from: http://www.bvda.com/EN/download/Gellifter_brochure_EN_2012.pdf

Center for Applied Science and Technology—CAST. (2014). *Fingermark visualisation manual.* Great Britain, Home Office: Center for Applied Science and Technology.

Collins, J., & Hussey, R. (2003). *Business research* (2nd ed.). New York: Palgrave.

Hammell, L., Deacon, P., & Farrugia, K. J. (2014). Chemical enhancement of soil-based marks on nonporous surfaces followed by gelatin lifting. *Journal of Forensic Identification, 64*(6), 583–608.

Kaboub, F. (2008). Positivist paradigm. In F. T. L. Leong (Ed.), *Encyclopedia of counseling* (p. 243). New York: Sage. Retrieved from: http://personal.denison.edu/~kaboubf/Pub/2008-Positivist-Paradigm.pdf

Milne, R. (2013). *Forensic intelligence*. Boca Raton: Taylor & Francis Group.

Patton, M. Q. (2002). *Qualitative research and evaluation methods*. Thousand Oaks: Sage.

Sollund, R., & Brisman, A. (2017). Editors' introduction to the special issue "researching environmental harm, doing green criminology". *Critical Criminology, 25*(2), 159–163.

Yin, R. K. (2009). *Case study research: Design and methods* (4th ed.). London: Sage.

Chapter 5
Findings

5.1 Chapter Preview

In this chapter, findings based on the (criteria of) analysis of ten gelatine lifters are presented (see Sect. 4.4). This chapter ends with a summary of the findings.

5.2 Conceptual Outline of the Presentation of Findings

The images of the gelatine lifters are presented and described with regard to the integrity of the image, the presence of any finger/footwear marks and the indications on survivability from the pilot.

5.3 Presentation of Ten Samples

Sample 1: Footprint on floor (tiles), indoor (Fig. 5.1)

1. *Description of the location*: Sample 1 shows a footprint taken from tiles within a farmhouse. The floor was cool and shady. The tiles were smooth.
2. *Surface description*: Smooth, non-porous, non-permeating surface.
3. *Integrity of the image*: The integrity of the image is good; the footprint shows clearly defined surface contours from the donor surface. The edges are medium strong and medium focused. The scans are generally clear and trace material is visible in the image.
4. *Presence of marks*: The footwear marks are visible and good. Particularly the ridges are present on the gelatine lifters, as expected with regard to the surface.

C.-H. Mayer, *Combating Wildlife Crime in South Africa*, SpringerBriefs in Criminology, https://doi.org/10.1007/978-3-030-05891-3_5

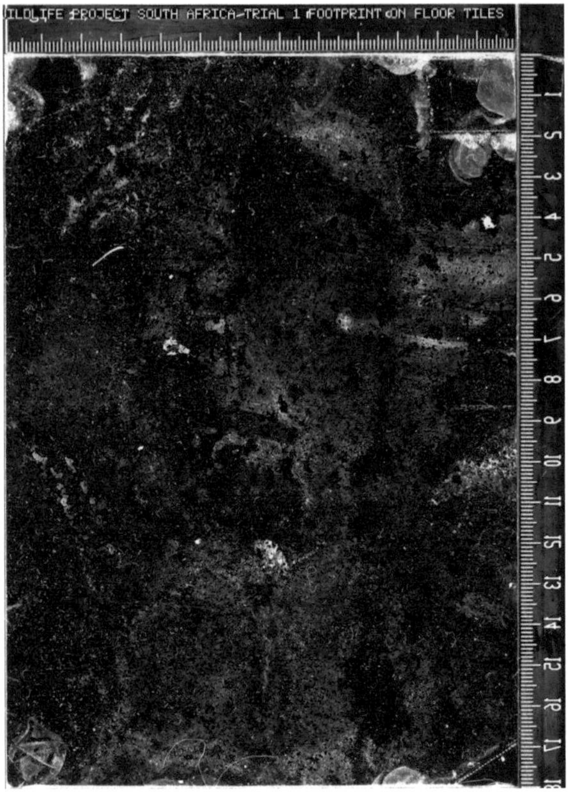

Fig. 5.1 Footprint on floor (tiles), indoor

5. *Indications on survivability from the pilot*: The gelatine lifters were in good condition; there was no obvious degradation due to heat. If there had been, one would see bright patches in the image where the detail had been obscured. Furthermore during transit, trace materials remained and were contained within the box.

Sample 2: Fingerprint on wood, indoor (Fig. 5.2)

1. *Description of the location*: Sample 2 shows a fingerprint taken from a wooden surface within a farmhouse. The wood was in a cool, dry and shady place. The tiles were smooth.
2. *Surface description*: Smooth, non-porous, non-permeating surface.
3. *Integrity of the image*: The integrity of the image is very good. The surface contours are clearly defined from the donor surface, the edges are strong and focused, the scan is remarkably clear and trace materials are visble in the image.
4. *Presence of marks*: The fingerprint is visible and good. In particular, the ridges of the fingers are present on the gelatine lifters, as to be expected with regard to the surface.

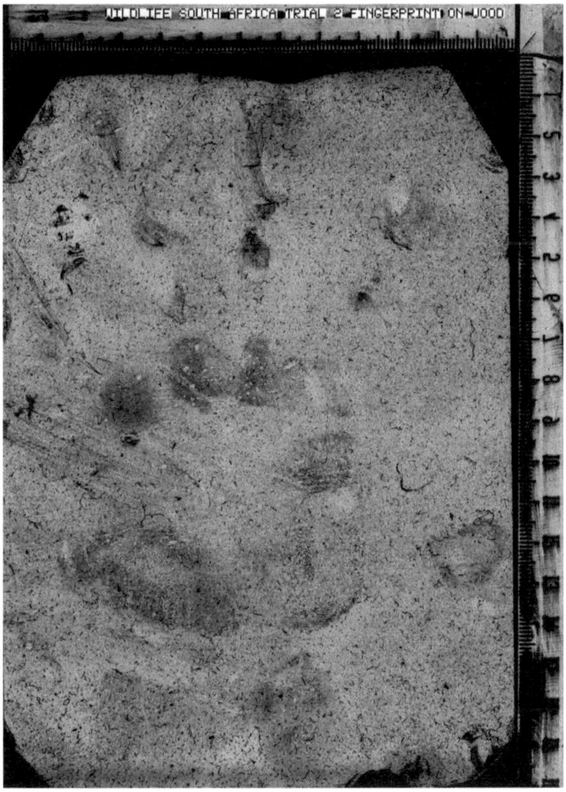

Fig. 5.2 Fingerprint on wood, indoor

5. *Indications on survivability from the pilot*: The remote recovery and dissemination of the gels are achievable.

Sample 3: Footprint on floor (tiles), indoor (Fig. 5.3)

1. *Description of the location*: Sample 3 shows a footprint taken from tiles within a farmhouse. The floor was cool and shady. The tiles were smooth.
2. *Surface description*: Smooth, non-porous, non-permeating surface.
3. *Integrity of the image*: The integrity of the image is good with distortions. The surface contours are partly defined from the donor surface, and the edges are not very strong and are not focused. The scan is only medium clear. Trace materials are visible in the image.
4. *Presence of marks*: The footprints are visible and good. In particular, the ridges are present on the gelatine lifters, as expected with regard to the surface.
5. *Indications on survivability from the pilot*: The remote recovery and dissemination of the gels are achievable.

Fig. 5.3 Footprint on floor (tiles), indoor

Sample 4: Fingerprint on stone (outdoor area) (Fig. 5.4)

1. *Description of the location*: Sample 4 shows a fingerprint taken from a stony surface in an outdoor area on a farmland. The stone area was cool and shady. The stone surface was rough.
2. *Surface description*: Rough, porous surface, non-permeating surface.
3. *Integrity of the image*: The integrity of the image is good but shows distortions. The surface contours and edges are not clearly defined and are not focused. Accordingly, the scan is also not clear and trace materials are only partly visible.
4. *Presence of marks*: The fingerprints are hardly visible and are of poor quality, as can be expected with regard to the surface description.
5. *Indications on survivability from the pilot*: The remote recovery and dissemination of the gels are achievable.

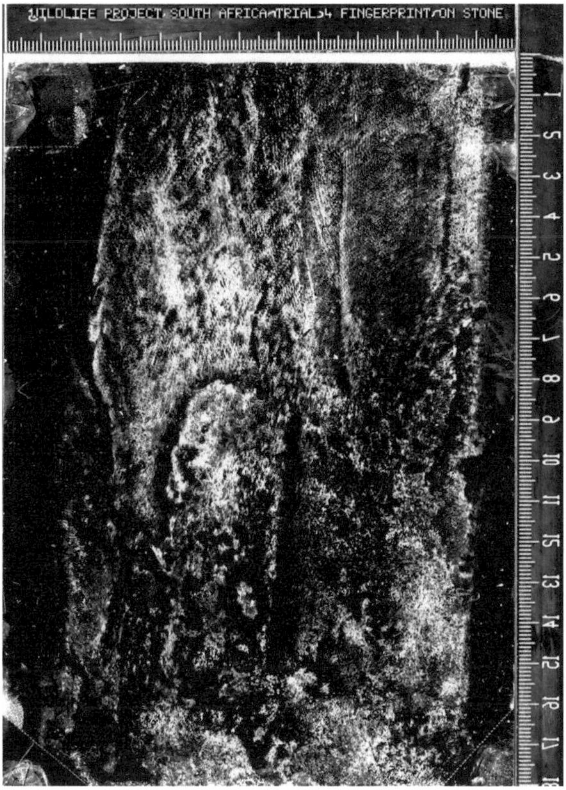

Fig. 5.4 Fingerprint on stone, outdoor area

Sample 5: Shoeprint on woodbench (outdoor area) (Fig. 5.5)

1. *Description of the location*: Sample 5 shows a shoeprint taken from a wooden surface (a bench) in an outdoor area on a farm land. The wooden area was cool and shady. The bench surface was smooth.
2. *Surface description*: Smooth, non-porous, non-permeating surface.
3. *Integrity of the image*: The integrity of the image is very good. It shows clearly defined surface contours from the donor surface, strong and focused edges, a generally clear scan as well as trace material.
4. *Presence of marks*: The shoeprints are very visible and very good, as to be expected with regard to the surface description.
5. *Indications on survivability from the pilot*: The remote recovery and dissemination of the gels are achievable.

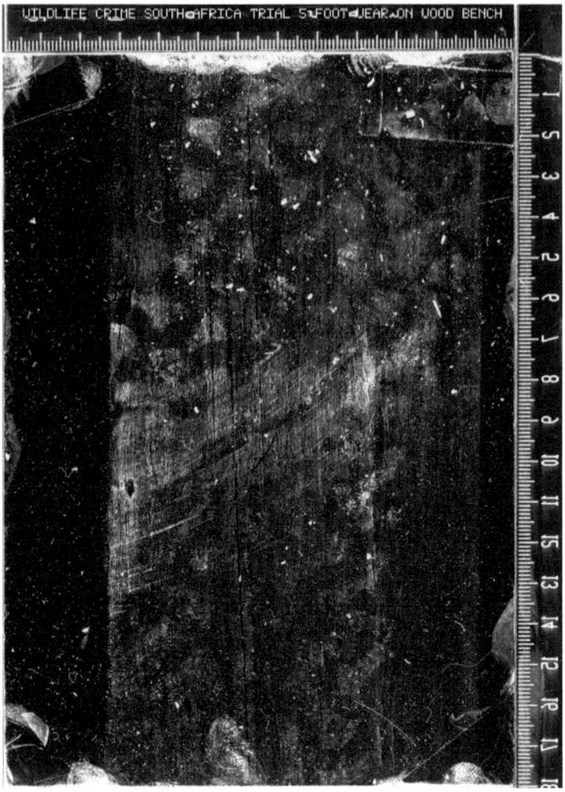

Fig. 5.5 Shoeprint on woodbench, outdoor area

Sample 6: Handprint on plastic bin (outdoor area) (Fig. 5.6)

1. *Description of the location*: Sample 6 shows a handprint taken from a plastic bin surface in an outdoor area on a farm land. The plastic bin was standing in a sunny, dry and warm area.
2. *Surface description*: Rough, porous, non-permeating surface.
3. *Integrity of the image*: The integrity of the image is good with distortions, it is moderately clearly defined and the surface contours are visible. However, the image shows weak and unfocused edges. The scan is clear and trace materials are visible.
4. *Presence of marks*: The handprints are visible and of good quality, particularly when taking the rough and porous surface in a warm area into account.
5. *Indications on survivability from the pilot*: The remote recovery and dissemination of the gels are achievable.

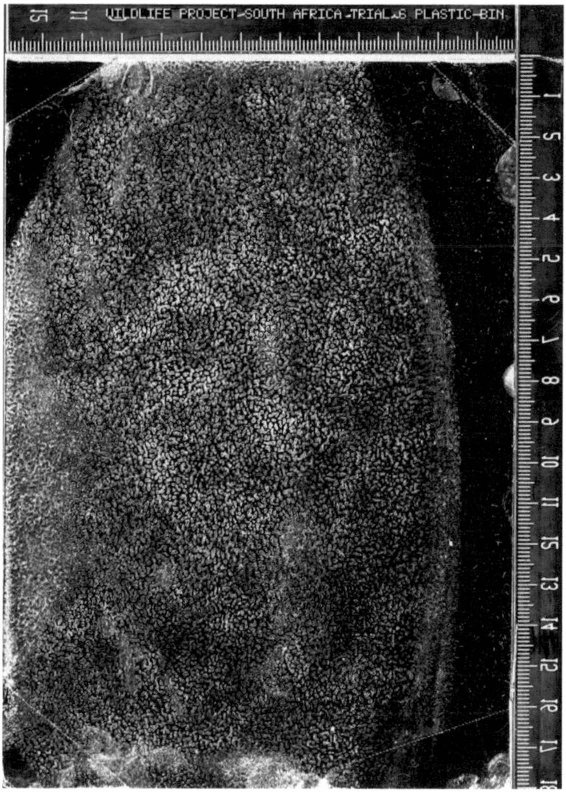

Fig. 5.6 Handprint on plastic bin, outdoor area

Sample 7: Footprint on stone area—farmland, outdoor, sunny and hot area (Fig. 5.7)

1. *Description of the location*: Sample 7 shows a footprint taken from a stony surface in an outdoor area on a farmland. The stone area was sunny and hot during the day time in South African spring with temperatures up to 32 °C on that day in this area. The stone surface was rough.
2. *Surface description*: Rough, porous, non-permeating surface.
3. *Integrity of the image*: The integrity of the image is good with distortions, the surface contours are partly defined and the edges are rather weak and unfocused. The scan is medium clear and trace materials are visible in the image.
4. *Presence of marks*: The footprint is visible and of quite good quality, particularly with regard to the heat and the stony and porous surface.
5. *Indications on survivability from the pilot*: The remote recovery and dissemination of the gels are achievable.

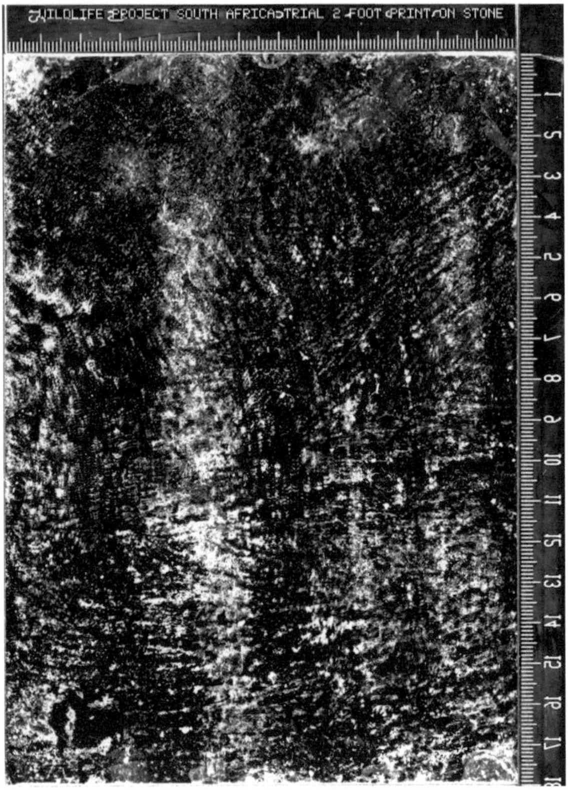

Fig. 5.7 Footprint on stone area—farmland, outdoor, sunny and hot area

Sample 8: Fingerprint on magazine paper, outdoor area, sunny and hot area (Fig. 5.8)

1. *Description of the location*: Sample 8 shows a fingerprint taken from a magazine (paper) surface which was lying in an outdoor area on a farm land in a sunny and hot place. The paper was placed in a sunny, hot and dry spot on a table. The paper surface was smooth.
2. *Surface description*: Smooth, non-porous, non-permeating.
3. *Integrity of the image*: The integrity of the image is good with distortions and the surface contours are partly defined. The edges are not strong and are not focused. The scan, however, is clear and trace material is visible in the image.
4. *Presence of marks*: The fingerprints are visible; however, there is little attrition in quality, and the detail can be observed, as might be expected with the surface description and the temperature.
5. *Indications on survivability from the pilot*: The remote recovery and dissemination of the gels are achievable.

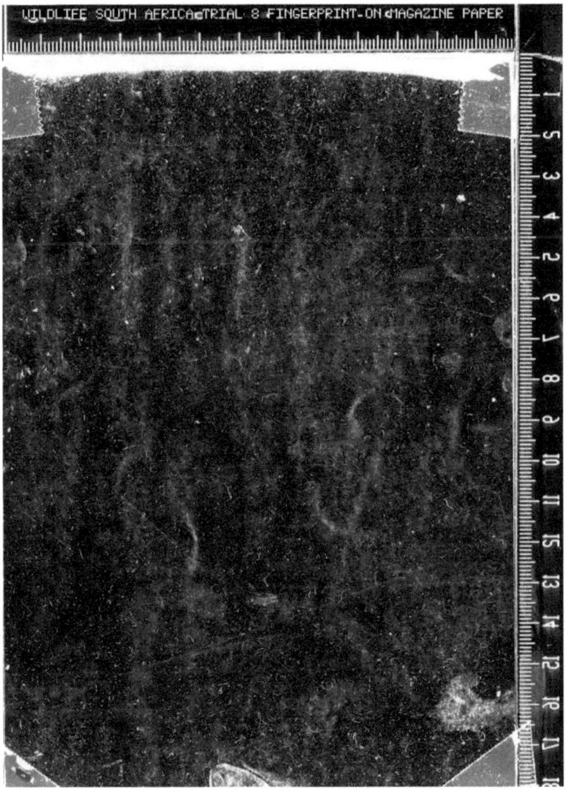

Fig. 5.8 Fingerprint on magazine paper, outdoor area, sunny and hot area

Sample 9: Fingerprint on metal lamp, inside area, sunny (Fig. 5.9)

1. *Description of the location*: Sample 9 shows a fingerprint taken from a metal lamp surface in an inside area of a farmhouse. The metal lamp was standing in a sunny, dry area within the house. The metal itself was cool and smooth on the surface.
2. *Surface description*: Smooth, non-porous, non-permeating.
3. *Integrity of the image*: The integrity of the image is good and has partly clearly defined surface contours from the donor surface. The edges are medium strong and focused, the scan is clear and the trace materials are visible in the image.
4. *Presence of marks*: The fingerprints are visible and of good quality, as might be expected with regard to the surface description.
5. *Indications on survivability from the pilot*: The remote recovery and dissemination of the gels are achievable.

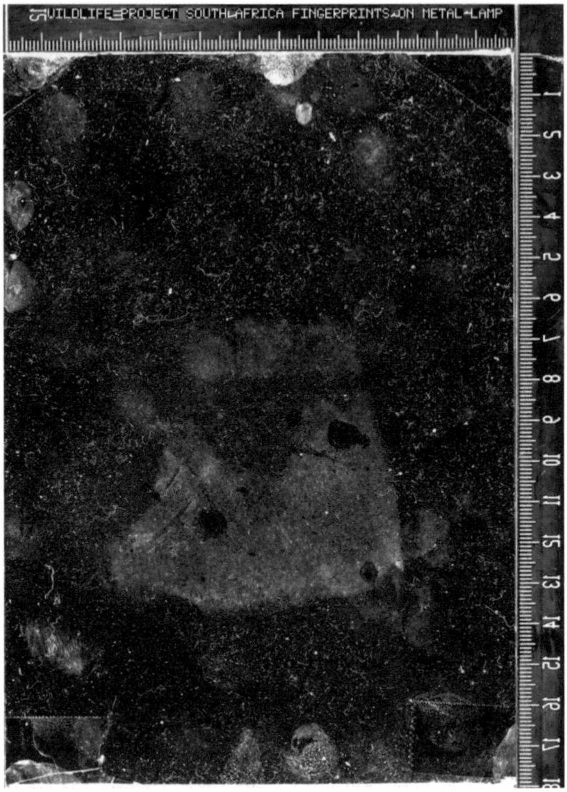

Fig. 5.9 Fingerprint on metal lamp, inside area, sunny

Sample 10: Fingerprint on wood cupboard, vertical, indoor area, cool place (Fig. 5.10)

1. *Description of the location*: Sample 10 shows a fingerprint taken from a wooden, vertical surface in an indoor area in a farm house. The wooden cupboard area was cool and shady. The wood surface was smooth.
2. *Surface description*: Smooth, non-porous, non-permeating.
3. *Integrity of the image*: The integrity of the image is very good, the surface is clearly defined regarding surface contours from the donor surface. The edges are strong and focused and the scan is very clear. The trace material is visible in the image.
4. *Presence of marks*: The fingerprints are clearly visible and of good quality, as might be expected with regard to the surface description.
5. *Indications on survivability from the pilot*: The remote recovery and dissemination of the gels are achievable.

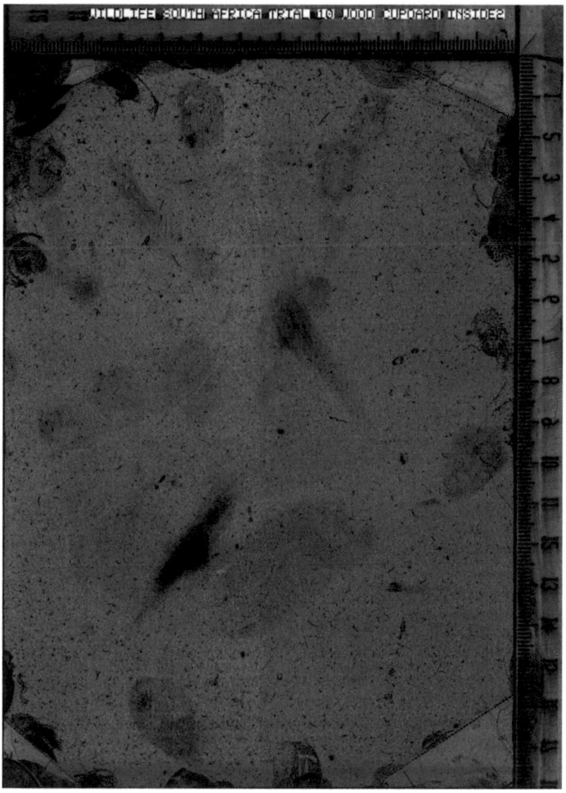

Fig. 5.10 Fingerprint on wood cupboard, vertical, indoor area, cool place

5.4 Summary of the Findings with Regard to the Ten Samples

Summarising, it can be emphasised that the surface of the donor source was either smooth, rough or non-porous (see Table 5.1). All the surfaces were non-permeating. The integrity of the images was three times very good (2, 5, 10), two times good (1, 9), five times good with distortions (3, 4, 6, 7, 8) and not poor at all. The presence of the marks varied from very good (5, 10), good (1, 2, 3, 6, 7, 9) to poor (4). There was no image which did not show any mark. Indications on survivability from the pilot show good recovery and dissemination of the gels which are achievable. The surface continuity does not exhibit attrition in detail showing fingerprints on all images. Generally, no visible decline in the quality of the image due to couriering and laboratory processing could be seen. In case of poor marks in terms of presence of distortions in the integrity of the image, the attrition can be related to the rough porous surface (such as stone or plastic). The initial assumption of remote lifting supported by courier and laboratory processing has been supported, even when using gelatine lifters in 32 °C heat.

Table 5.1 General overview of findings

No.	Location	Surface: non-porous, smooth, rough, porous, permeating	Integrity of image: very good, good, good with distortions, no image	Presence of marks: very good, good, poor, no marks	Indications on survivability from the pilot
1	Indoor smooth cold tiles	Smooth, non-porous, non-permeating	Good, clear surface contours, the edges are medium strong and medium focused, clear surface, trace material is visible in image	Good, in particular ridges of footprint are visible	Recovery and dissemination of the gels are achievable
2	Indoor, smooth, cold wooden surface	Smooth, non-porous, non-permeating	Very good, very clear surface contours, the edges are strong and focused, very clear surface, trace material is visible in image	Good, particularly ridges of fingerprint are visible	Recovery and dissemination of the gels are achievable
3	Indoor, smooth cold tiles	Smooth, non-porous, non-permeating	Good with distortions, contours are partly defined, the edges are not very strong and focused and the scan is medium clear. Trace materials are visible in image	Good, particularly ridges of footprint are visible	Recovery and dissemination of the gels are achievable
4	Outdoor area, cool stone	Rough, porous surface, non-permeating	Good with distortions, unclear surface contours, hardly defined, not strong edges, unclear scan and trace materials are only partly visible	Hardly visible with poor marks	Recovery and dissemination of the gels are achievable
5	Outdoor area, cool, woodbench	Smooth, non-porous, non-permeating	Very good, very clearly defined surface contours from the donor surface, strong and focused edges, a generally clear scan as well as trace material is well visible in the image	Very good	Recovery and dissemination of the gels are achievable
6	Outdoor area, warm, plastic bin	Rough, porous surface, non-permeating	Good with distortions medium clearly defined, the surface contours are visible; image does show weak and edges are not clearly focused; the scan is clear and trace materials are visible	Good	Recovery and dissemination of the gels are achievable
7	Outdoor area, sunny and hot, stone surface	Rough, porous surface, non-permeating	Good with distortions, the surface contours are partly defined and the edges are rather weak and unfocused. The scan is medium clear and trace materials are visible in the image	Good	Recovery and dissemination of the gels are achievable

8	Outdoor area, sunny and hot, magazine on table, paper surface	Smooth, non-porous, non-permeating	Good with distortions and the surface contours are partly defined, the edges are not strong and not focused. Clear scan and trace material is visible in the image	Good the fingerprints are visible; however, there is a little attrition in quality and the ridge detail can be observed	Recovery and dissemination of the gels are achievable
9	Indoor area, sunny, metal lamp surface (cool on surface)	Smooth, non-porous, non-permeating	Good, partly clearly defined surface contours from the donor surface, the edges are medium strong and focused, the scan is clear and the trace materials are visible in the image	Good	Recovery and dissemination of the gels are achievable
10	Indoor area, wood cupboard, vertical, cool surface	Smooth, non-porous, non-permeating	Very good, the surface is clearly defined regarding surface contours, the edges are strong and focused and the scan is very clear; the trace mateiral is visible in the image	Very good	Recovery and dissemination of the gels are achievable

Source: Author's own construction

5.5 Chapter Summary

This chapter described the findings of ten samples analysed based on predefined analysis criteria. The findings are provided as figures and verbal descriptions and show that gelatine lifters can be used and couriered over long distances without losing quality with regard to marks recovered on the gelatine lifters during laboratory processing.

Chapter 6
Discussion, Conclusions and Recommendations

6.1 Chapter Preview

Findings are discussed in accordance with the literature presented in Chaps. 2 and 3 in order to provide a comprehensive discourse on the subject researched. Conclusions are provided, and recommendations for future research and context-specific forensic operational practice are presented.

6.2 Discussing the Findings in Context

Since wildlife crime is of a growing global and Pan-African concern (Wilson-Wilde, 2010, p. 221; Ayling, 2013; Nellemann, Henriksen, Raxter, Ash, & Mrema, 2014), this study contributes to evaluating the functionality and performance of the forensic method using gelatine lifters for forensic intelligence through combating (international) wildlife crime. It is being anchored in the field of green criminology and evaluates the use, suitability and performance of the lifters described for the visualisation and sequential processing of prints and environmental traces, thereby contributing to the increasing international research in trace recovery, whilst addressing research voids (as in Wellsmith, 2011).

Findings show that traces taken by the forensic method of gelatine lifting for forensic enabled intelligence within South Africa show very good results. This is of particular importance, since the traces on gelatine lifters were shipped long distances to be evaluated. Findings show that gelatine lifters worked well under various environmental conditions (e.g. temperature, indoor and outdoor areas, different surface materials). Conclusions and recommendation for theory and practice are presented after the benefits of research are discussed.

C.-H. Mayer, *Combating Wildlife Crime in South Africa*, SpringerBriefs in Criminology, https://doi.org/10.1007/978-3-030-05891-3_6

6.2.1 International Cooperation to Combat Wildlife Crime

This study is a well-established example of an international research project conducted in tight cooperation between researchers, investigators and forensic specialists, as Wilson-Wilde (2010) emphasised as necessary to combat wildlife crime effectively. It is concerned with the South African perspective (South African Development Community, 2015; South & Wyatt, 2011; Wyatt, 2009), thereby emphasising the need for a deeper understanding of the contextual challenges to combat wildlife crime within the described context. This work provides further support for previous research (e.g. Lunstrum, 2014) highlighting the urgent need for international collaboration and action against the criminal networks. This is to be achieved not only through "green militarisation" but also from a strategic and operational viewpoint which counteracts against the strengths, flexibility and ruthlessness of criminal networks by using forensic investigation tools.

6.2.2 Pan-African and Far East Cooperation

International stakeholders—particularly China, Russia or the USA (Taylor, Lindsey, & Davies-Mostert, 2016) where the biggest seizures of ivory/horn were found (Biggs, Courchamp, Martin, & Possingham, 2013)—should focus on decreasing the demand for wildlife hunting through educational and training programmes. These should not only include the consequences on socio-economic, biological and environment levels but also in terms of crime studies in order to establish wildlife crime as a "serious international crime" (see Sect. 2.4). Only then will wildlife crime be recognised, treated effectively, and more monetary funds and resources will be allocated for improved research and operational practice.

Consequently, national laws and restrictions within these countries need to be changed, and culture-specific programmes to combat wildlife crime need to be established. The well-established legal economic trades between African countries and the Far East (e.g. between China and South Africa) should further be used to combat illegal wildlife trade, and research networks on wildlife crime between these regions should be established.

Further, culturalisations and cultural stereotyping with regard to Asian criminal networks (see Lambrechts & Goga, 2016) should not distract from the focus on Pan-African wildlife crime and the intra-African criminal networks. Multiple criminal networks, inter- and intra-continental, should be focused on similarly and ivory/horn seized in transit needs to be collected, analysed and evaluated, and data on illegal trade and criminal networks (such as established through forensic investigations with gelatine lifters) need to be stored and internationally made available. In this context, valid international/Pan-African law enforcement practices need to be established along with the investigation processes.

6.2.3 Acknowledging and Addressing South African Specifics and (Post-)apartheid Influences

Since wildlife in South Africa is declared as being "common property" (Snijders, 2015, p. 15), a common, public and systemic approach is needed to address wildlife crime. Although wildlife-based tourism is an important factor of the South African economy (Michel et al., 2006), its central role is still neglected by governmental institutions (Snijders, 2015). This study strengthens the central role of wildlife in South Africa through its focus within a research-based educational context, thus highlighting the importance of wildlife for the country and requesting it to be made a key political concern.

For combating wildlife crime effectively, South Africa's colonialisation and apartheid history needs to be considered as a strong influencing factor. Apartheid has led to a still "untransformed" society in which members of certain groups struggle for survival, acknowledgement and rights. From international and interdisciplinary perspectives (history, human rights, social sciences, humanities), human solutions for South Africa's "previously disadvantaged groups" (NAMC, 2006) need to be found, for building sustainable solutions for wildlife/animals, since local communities will only protect animals, if human needs for survival and (self-) respect are satisfied (Tapela & Omara-Ojungu, 1999). Bushmeat trade will also decrease (Lindsey & Taylor, 2012) when marginalisation of these groups decreases (Lambrechts & Goga, 2016). This study suggests that the fulfilment of these needs can be addressed through culture- and context-specific educational and training programmes on protecting wildlife which take different system levels (cognitive, behavioural and psychosocial/emotional) of learning into account.

Wildlife crime will only be sustainably defeated if individual and sociocultural group dynamics in South Africa are taken seriously. Thus it is assumed that wildlife protection needs to become a local and public concern and an anticipated long-term change of societal norms and human values and behaviour. This might—if well conducted—lead to an increase in ownership and agency of the local communities to taking up wildlife protection and ranching and a deeper governmental interest, resulting in local, regional and national governmental wildlife protection programmes and the needed restructuring of private-/government-owned wildlife conservation (Ashley & Wolmer, 2003). Within these socio-economic restructuring processes, ownership of combating wildlife crime and interest in forensic investigation processes might be established.

6.2.4 Bottom-Up and Top-Down Approaches in South Africa

South Africa needs a two-pronged strategy of wildlife crime combat, by gaining the buy-in of local, provincial and regional communities (bottom-up approach) and national/international programmes (top-down approach). Training of professionals needs to increase, and competencies and expertise need to be developed (see also Damm, 2005; Snijders, 2012). At the same time, creating ownership and agency in laypersons (e.g. rangers, private security personnel) of local communities who share the habitats of the rural environments and who might be the first individuals to arrive at the crime scene is highly important.

Since there is an urgent need to protect wildlife and to combat wildlife crime, quick actions are needed, and the buy-in of local inhabitants of rural/remote areas are needed to ensure effective collaboration. Local key holders, such as elders within the community, need to be addressed in an culturally adequate way (e.g. speaking to the person in charge in local communities; knowing cultural rituals and traditional regulations to cooperate effectively; knowing local languages to ensure cooperation; providing the local, provincial, regional, national decision-makers with the right information; addressing them in a status-adequate way to build long-term relationships; etc.).

To effectively install the use of gelatine lifters, various actors and movements (green militarisation, legalising ivory/horn trade movements, security coordination, police forces, the South African ESPU, ECEC etc.) need to be included to counteract corruption and build networks of broad social responsibility. Actors within key positions in law enforcement need to be paid and trained effectively in order to fulfil their roles and become responsible network key holders in decentralised forensic investigation processes which comply with the centralised law enforcement and anti-poaching strategy (SADC, 2016–2021).

Governmental stakeholders and private landowners need to be increasingly convinced to "buy-into" wildlife conservation, e.g. through governmental subsidies and landowner-friendly changes of regulations (such as taxation laws) (e.g. Cloete, Van Der Merwe, & Saayman, 2015) which could be connected to obligatory educational and training courses on wildlife protection and crime combat. On micro- and meso-levels, provincial and regional conservation networks could be established to cooperate with representatives of regional/national governmental organisations, landowners associations, and NGOs (see also Brockington, Duffy, & Igoe, 2008) to focus not only on conservation and economic flourishing but also on the pro-active combat of wildlife crime. These multi-level conservation networks could support the effective use and implementation of forensic intervention tools and techniques during crime investigation.

Besides the addressed regional and provincial networks for conservation and the combat of wildlife crime, national and global networks (partners, stakeholders, governmental and international organisations and NGOs) should cooperate more effectively and flexibly in research, policies and programmes of action which address the needs of the local level (micro- and meso-) on a practical note.

6.2.5 *Developing Crime Studies and Interdisciplinary Perspectives on Wildlife Crime*

This study supports Snijders's (2015) argument, by contributing to research in the discipline of international crime studies and particularly in forensic investigation tool development. It also touches on the importance of re-adjusting wildlife laws and animal rights within the context of the law enforcement and anti-poaching strategy (SADC, 2016–2021).

This study states that wildlife crime combat needs an interdisciplinary perspective by taking into account the loss of biodiversity/environmental destruction (biological perspectives), the reasons for poaching for subsistence and commercial purposes (Ayling, 2013; Newmark & Hough, 2000) (economic perspectives), as well as the governmental legislation and policy (political perspectives) to reinforce and strengthen the importance of the topic. Thereby, the interdisciplinary perspectives need to be understood from systemic viewpoints, highlighting their complexity and multidimensionality, thus emphasising Ramutsindela's (2016) viewpoint. This study states consistently that an exclusively linear worldview to combat wildlife crime is insufficient and that a systemic and contextualising approach is incircumventable.

6.2.6 *(Training) Professionalism Using Investigative Tools*

This study shows that some parts of the forensic crime investigation processes (e.g. analysis in laboratories) need a high technological and professional standard, whilst the collection of data needs at minimum the expertise of forensic investigators to secure traces. The use of gelatine lifters within crime investigations is relatively simple to handle, and professionals need to be trained to develop a basic understanding of forensic investigation and crime scene interventions.

Training programmes need to be provided to prepare professional crime investigators to use forensic investigation tools (e.g. gelatine lifters). This training needs to include the entire process: how/where to order which investigation tools; how/where to store; how/where to use; how/where to pack, store, and mail the gelatine lifters; and how/where to receive evaluation access. Through professional training (using culture-specific education and African didactic curricula), investigation procedures should visualise the step-by-step process, e.g. using training material in local languages, working with pictures/posters to visualising processes, showing local impacts of wildlife crime and addressing social responsibility. These educational training processes for professionals might support an optimal and most effective use of forensic tools (from identifying the forensic tools needed for investigation at the scene to the access of the evaluated data). Professional training needs to be (made) available across the country and particularly in rural/remote areas. From a long-term perspective, the training will also contribute to developing best practices in law enforcement, intelligence and investigation and, further on, support the arguments in court cases (as emphasised in Henson, Malpas, & D'Udine, 2016).

6.2.7 Establishing Training Centres in Remote Areas

Training centres for crime scene investigations should be established in African countries, providing courses in investigation methods and use of investigation tools/ crime scene analysis. However, these training centres should also provide training for the "layperson" who works in crime scene-related professions (rangers, game farm worker, community representatives, private security, etc.). These individuals often arrive at crime scenes first and should be trained to assist the professionals by securing the crime scenes. They are also key holders in building bridges to the local communities which they usually belong to and can create awareness and help to establish the "buy-in" of the communities.

Training centres need to be established in the provinces where wildlife crime is likely to happen and in wildlife crime transit areas. These decentralised training centres should not only train relevant key actors but also strengthen the law enforcement capacities through motivational programmes to combat wildlife crime, recruiting key actors in the field, in-service training (see Henson et al., 2016) and the storage and provision of key equipment, such as forensic investigation tools (e.g. gelatine lifters). Law enforcement could be implemented through these training centres on a micro-level. These training centres could not only focus on wildlife crime but can also provide the communities with investigation tools which are used in human conflict/crime scenes. This "double effect" could support the buy-in of local communities.

Training centres need to use Africanised didactical approaches (see above) which is accepted and understood by local learners. "Robust procedures" as described by Henson et al. (2016) can only be one aspect of successful law enforcement. The so-called "self-selected" (Henson et al., 2016) intelligence officers need to be acknowledged and their role within the communities strengthened through professional training. If communal key actors can be identified, professional training can support the effectiveness of investigative processes. However, highly professional staff are also needed.

6.2.8 Professional Training in Higher Education Institutions (HEI)

Besides the inclusion of local key actors, the wildlife crime combat needs highly specialised intelligence investigation staff (Henson et al., 2016), researchers to develop culture-/context-specific investigation equipment and the establishment of competences on the spot.

In HEIs in African countries, degree paths in criminology, crime studies, criminal psychology, investigation, etc. need to be advanced in terms of bachelor/master/doctoral degrees and the status of studying these subjects needs to be established and heightened.

The attractiveness of the professional field of becoming an investigator/law enforcement professional needs to be established and strengthened by providing accessible career paths, public recognition and acknowledgement and a reasonable prospect of success, a highly acknowledged societal status and monetary compensation for working in a demanding and dangerous profession.

African researchers and professional law enforcement practitioners which are active need to be able to see their personal career development potential when deciding on a career path within this professional field. To act sustainably in long-term perspectives, the responsibilities for investigation processes need to be re-established within (South) African contexts, and African scholars and practitioners need to develop new ideas on self-responsibility for their societies and environments.

Furthermore, wildlife crime investigation as a professional field needs to undergo an image change in African countries—from a low paid, dangerous and corrupt professional field towards a highly compensated, internationally and locally recognised, high status profession. To implement this image change, technology and investigation analysis tools, as well as laboratories, need to be located in African countries to strengthen the importance of the field and to acknowledge local competences and skills. Thereby, the self-esteem of African researchers and professionals within this field will be strengthened, and this newly established self-esteem will attract capable individuals to the profession. In addition, the profession should be developed and presented as a professional field of the future with good job prospectus and technological progress.

With regard to these degree paths, close cooperation with governmental and private law enforcement units within African countries needs to be established to ensure intelligence to progress through locally based research and practical operational application, particularly in forensic crime investigation and intelligence.

HEI-based research on and application of gelatine lifters provides new contextualised information on crime syndicate operations, since the origin of ivory/horn can be determined and the forensic investigations do not only start at the point of shipping as in previous years (Wasser et al., 2008). This study provides an effective example of international cooperation and contributes to developing a well-functioning "collection kit" (Henson et al., 2016) on an applied and practical level, as well as with regard to "country-crossing" (see Wasser et al., 2008). It is also a good example for international HEI cooperation and for increasing established African-based research and investigation practice.

6.2.9 Developing the Use of Investigation Methods in Green Criminology

This study contributes to exploring identification methods used in tracing wildlife crime (as in Ogden, Dawnay, & McEwing, 2009) and provides one step forward in the milestone project of combating wildlife crime through identifying physical, biological, botanical and traded material by using gelatine lifters (as described in Sect. 3.3). It thereby contributes to the research on investigative methods in green criminology (e.g. Lynch, 1990; Lynch, Long, Stretesky, & Barrett, 2017; Moreto & Pires, 2018) and particularly wildlife crime (Cooper & Cooper, 2013). By taking the dangers at the crime scene into consideration (wildlife scene, natural habitat, local communities, etc.), evidence needs to be collected quickly, and traces collected need to be stored away without much effort. Gelatine lifters cater for all of these local needs, as shown in this study.

This study expands previous research methods of lifting prints with gelatine films (Wiesner, Tsach, Belser, & Shor, 2011; Sect. 3.3) and provides support for previous studies:

(a) Traces lifted with gelatine markers can be simply and quickly collected through the application of the gel (even through non-professional individuals).
(b) Traces on gelatine markers can be shipped abroad without/with little damage/without visible or recognisable loss of data or trace information.
(c) The laboratory analysis can be conducted abroad, in a well-equipped laboratory, if a responsible mail service is used,
(d) Evaluated data can be returned to the country of evidence collection (at least into areas where there is electricity and internet connection) through computerised systems/electronic databases.

The ability to send the collected evidence over great distances means that key actors can store the equipment in a centralised area and employ the appropriate experts to send evidence abroad. Furthermore, the ability to analyse traces which have built up on the samples over time offers greater evidential value in terms of long-term investigation processes.

This study contributes to previous tests (see Sect. 3.3) that gelatine lifters are functional/effective, even under the described harsh environmental conditions. The study therefore supports the overall intrinsic investigative value of gelatine lifters through the successful exploration of extrinsic trace evidence.

In addition to this, gelatine lifters support exploring the strategies of criminal networks in more depth in terms of how they cooperate (network structures/operational strategies). Therefore, this study contributes to the study of Wasser et al. (2008), emphasising the importance of genetic forensic tools exploration in crime studies.

6.2.10 Culture-Specifics in Investigation Processes

The implementation of "Western" forensic processes and use of tools needs culturally adequate implementation in African countries so as not to clash with local and culture-specific rules and regulations, norms and values. Furthermore, explanations of the necessity of these tools, their value and importance need to be described and explained in a culturally comprehensible and acceptable way to ensure compliance of (South) African professionals as well as the layperson who might be involved in the investigation processes. The impact (and collective wounds) of colonialisation, imperialisation and apartheid (in South Africa particularly) should not be underestimated. Often international collaboration faces challenges due to the historic impacts in communication processes, intercultural prejudices or stereotypes and/or unacknowledged (psychological) injuries.

African investigation professionals (or even rangers, frontline researchers, private security company professionals, landowners, etc.) who might become involved in securing traces using forensic investigation tools at crime scenes value communication with Western professionals which is based on a dialogue of equals between the two cultures or professions. Attitudes including arrogance and/or unfriendliness often impede intercultural effective collaboration.

6.2.11 Creating Public Awareness on Situation via Media

"Poaching and human-wildlife conflict" (Taylor et al., 2016) need to gain attention in the media (TV, news, new social media, etc.), thereby creating global awareness and consciousness with regard to the urgency of the issue. Furthermore, the significance of wildlife crime needs to be communicated in comparison with awareness, for example, it needs to be addressed with the similar attention and urgency as illegal drug trade (South & Wyatt, 2011). Additionally, it needs to be acknowledged publicly that wildlife crime has advanced to a state of organised crime (Wyatt, 2009) in order to receive adequate (inter-)national resources. Furthermore, the "endangered" status of elephants and rhinoceros needs to be acknowledged (South African Development Community, 2015) to underline the urgency of action needed as emphasised in this study.

(Media) campaigns should not only address the urgency of action needed but also present the appropriate ways forward, through creating public awareness that investigation tools, such as gelatine lifters, and effective tools to finally win the fight against wildlife crime are available.

Various representatives from governmental backgrounds, but also, e.g. celebrities, actors, singers, etc. need to be included in the (media) wildlife crime combat campaign to create consciousness from the top. At the same time, the media should address the concerns and needs at the local levels (bottom-up) to establish a concern for wildlife crime through all societal levels, whilst presenting possible solutions, for example, through simply applied investigative methods.

6.2.12 *Addressing Local Problems Through New Discourses and Actions*

Problems which counteract wildlife crime combat, such as corruption and low law enforcement discourses (Bennett, 2015; Harvey, 2016), need to be explored anew and common solutions need to be found across disciplines and nations. Discourses on how to deal with corruption in wildlife crime investigation and research/practice on how to explore bridges of legal and illegal markets (including actors involved, behaviours of actors, relationships with legal and illegal trading networks, involvement of legal partners such as police, military, special law enforcement and border protection units) need to be led. In this context, law enforcement measures and criminal justice interventions need to be installed and their role within the combat processes researched (see Hübschle, 2016). Gelatine lifters can in future bring "evidence destined for court" (Ogden et al., 2009) and thereby strengthen law enforcement in African contexts.

On all levels, despite strategy plans having been discussed and convention papers released (see Sect. 2.4), actions fail. The use of gelatine lifters is a practical, action-based approach and portrays a milestone in forensic investigation in wildlife crime in African countries. Forensic investigation methods can become the needed link between theories and practices, since they are simple to use and, if correctly used, provide a significant message.

Based on these identified benefits, recommendations for future research and operational practice are provided below.

6.3 Recommendations for Future Research and Operational Practice

Based on the findings of this study, future research on wildlife crime should be based in green criminology whilst following an interdisciplinary and systemic approach, tackling the void of research identified earlier in this study (e.g. Warchol & Johnson, 2011), such as illegal hunting and culture-specific views on wildlife (crime). In the following, recommendations for future research and operational practice will be given.

6.3.1 Recommendations for Future Research in Green Criminology

In future, green criminology can remain one of the frameworks for research on wildlife crime and combat whilst using intra- and interdisciplinary approaches in (green) criminology, combined with crime science and cultural studies.

Research needs to focus on exploring criminal network operations on local, provincial, regional, national, Pan-African and international levels to understand the illegal trading networks and methods on all levels. This can be done through further research in forensic investigation tools and their context- and culture-specific application which help to trace criminal network operations across African countries. Researchers need to cooperate closely with local communities, as well as local law enforcement, and need to research local approaches in forensic investigation, the context-specific application of investigation tools, such as gelatine lifters at crime scenes.

Research can focus on behaviour of professional crime scene investigators and law enforcement professionals in African countries, their attitudes, values and behaviour towards wildlife protection and wildlife crime. This should also be researched in local communities, as well as in key actors in the communities who might support the processes of investigation and the combat of wildlife crime.

Professional training in investigative strategies, crime studies, criminal psychology/behaviour and related fields needs to be analysed and evaluated through research. Thereby, the contextual and cultural fit of the trainings and courses needs to be studied to finally reach the highest level of compliance of professionals, layperson and community key actors in the fight against wildlife crime. Furthermore, best practices of training laypersons and community key role players on supporting the crime scene investigations in remote and rural areas should be developed. Training material—based on research—needs to be developed to create awareness on all societal levels, and materials should be translated into the most common African languages. Professional trainers from Western countries need to undergo culture-specific training in order to reach the highest compliance from African professionals, laypersons and community key actors.

On another note, the image of wildlife crime investigation/crime studies and related fields should be explored, and studies should focus on the necessity of image change with regard to the professions working towards wildlife crime reduction.

Finally, more research is needed to explore the use of gelatine lifters in different African contexts and settings with expanded sample sizes, in different African environmental contexts and with regard to the challenges professionals/laypersons and community key actors experience in applying simple forensic investigation tools at crime studies (e.g. in terms of storage, low technology, a void of labs, transport of samples, application of gelatine lifters in heat/rain seasons, etc.).

Studies should explore how databases should be built up to reach the best possible communication across global networks to distribute the forensic investigation data evaluations in countries across the world. Best practices need to be developed through research and the evaluation of practices with regard to dealing with the information gained through forensic investigation processes.

6.3.2 Recommendations for Operational Practice

In terms of the implications for operational practice, best practices—maybe even best practice models—should be developed with regard to:

(a) The application of forensic investigation tools at crime scenes in African countries
(b) The development of training materials (readers, books, posters, videos, theatre plays, stories) for professionals, laypersons and community key actors to effectively use investigative tools, e.g. gelatine lifters, in most common local languages
(c) Creating awareness and consciousness of wildlife protection and wildlife crime combat on all societal and international levels
(d) Communication and information sharing regarding evaluations of data collected

These best practices need to be implemented on global, regional, national and local levels to be sustainable in the long term.

6.4 Chapter Summary

The outcome of this research contributes to the understanding and the improvement of applied wildlife crime research and practice. It provides new information, reflects on applied theories and provides recommendations for future research and practice.

References

Ashley, C., & Wolmer, W. (2003). *Transforming or tinkering?: New forms of engagement between communities and the private sector in tourism and forestry in Southern Africa. Sustainable livelihoods in Southern Africa Programme*. Sussex: University of Sussex.

Ayling, J. (2013). What sustains wildlife crime? Rhino horn trading and the resilience of criminal networks. *Journal of International Wildlife Law & Policy, 16*, 57–80.

Bennett, E. L. (2015). Legal ivory trade in a corrupt world and its impact on African elephant populations. *Conservation Biology, 29*(1), 54–60.

Biggs, D., Courchamp, F., Martin, R., & Possingham, H. P. (2013). Conservation. Legal trade of Africa's rhino horns. *Science, 339*, 1038–1039.
Brockington, D., Duffy, R., & Igoe, J. (2008). *Nature unbound: Conservation, capitalism and the future of protected areas*. London: Routledge.
Cloete, P. C., Van Der Merwe, P., & Saayman, M. (2015). *Game ranch profitability in South Africa* (2nd ed.). Pretoria: Caxton.
Cooper, J. E., & Cooper, M. E. (Eds.). (2013). *Wildlife forensic investigation—principles and practice*. Boca Raton: CRC Press.
Damm, G. (2005). Hunting in South Africa: Facts, risks and opportunities. *African Indaba, 3*, 1–14.
Harvey, R. (2016). Risks and fallacies associated with promoting a legalised trade in Ivory. *Politikon, 43*(2), 215–229.
Henson, D. W., Malpas, R. C., & D'Udine, F. A. C. (2016). *Wildlife law enforcement in Sub-Saharan African protected areas. A review of best practices*. Cambridge, UK: International Union for Conservation of Nature and Natural Resources.
Hübschle, A. (2016). Security coordination in an illegal market: the transnational trade in rhinoceros horn. Politikon: South African Journal of Political Studies, *43*(2), 193–214.
Lambrechts, D., & Goga, K. (2016). Money and margitalisation: The lost war against Abalone poaching in South Africa. *Politikon, 43*(2), 231–249.
Lindsey, P.A., & Taylor, W.A. (2012). A study on the dehorning of African rhinoceroses as a tool to reduce the risk of poaching. Pretoria, South Africa: Department of Environmental Affairs.
Lunstrum, E. (2014). Green militarization: Anti-poaching efforts and the spatial contours of Kruger National Park. *Nature and Society, 104*(4), 816–832.
Lynch, M. J. (1990). The greening of criminology: A perspective on the 1990s. *The Critical Criminologist, 2*(3), 11–12.
Lynch, M. L., Long, M. A., Stretesky, P. B., & Barrett, K. L. (2017). *Green criminology. Crime, justice and the environment*. Oakland, CA: University of California Press.
Michel, A. L., Bengis, R. G., Hofmeyr, M., de Klerk, L. M., Cross, P. C., Jolles, A. E., et al. (2006). Wildlife tuberculosis in South African conservation areas: Implications and challenges. *Veterinary Microbiology, 112*(2–4), 91–100.
Moreto, W. D., & Pires, S. F. (2018). Wildlife crime. An environmental criminology and crime science perspective. Durham, NC: Carolina Academic Press.
Nellemann, C., Henriksen, R., Raxter, P., Ash, N., & Mrema, E. (2014). *The environmental crime crisis: Threats to sustainable development from illegal exploitation and trade in wildlife and forest resources*. Nairobi, Kenya: UN Environment Programme.
Newmark, W. D., & Hough, J. L. (2000). Conserving wildlife in Africa: Integrating conservation and development projects and beyond: Because multiple factors hinder integrated conservation and development projects in Africa from achieving their objectives, alternative and complementary approaches for promoting wildlife conservation must be actively explored. *BioScience, 50*(7), 585–592.
Ogden, R., Dawnay, N., & McEwing, R. (2009). Wildlife DNA forensics—bridging the gap between conservation genetics and law enforcement. *Endangered Species Research, 9*, 179–195.
Ramutsindela, M. (2016). Wildlife crime and state security in South(ern) Africa: An overview of developments. *Politikon, 43*(2), 159–171.
Snijders, D. (2012). Wild property and its boundaries—on wildlife policy and rural consequences in South Africa. *The Journal of Peasant Studies, 39*(2), 503–520.
Snijders, D. (2015). *Shifting species in South Africa. Wildlife policy, rural consequences* (Doctoral dissertation). University of Amsterdam. Retrieved from: http://www.rhinoresourcecenter.com/pdf_files/142/1422583600.pdf
South African Development Community. (2015). *Law enforcement and anti-poaching strategy*. Retrieved from: http://www.gaborone.diplo.de/contentblob/4715602/Daten/6225475/SADC_LEAP_FINAL.pdf

South, N., & Wyatt, T. (2011). Comparing illicit trades in wildlife and drugs: An exploratory study. *Deviant Behaviour, 32*(6), 538–361.
Tapela, B. N., & Omara-Ojungu, P. H. (1999). Towards bridging the gap between wildlife conservation and rural development in post-apartheid South Africa: The case of the Makulele community and the Kruger National Park. *South African Geographical Journal, 81*(3), 148–155.
Taylor, A., Lindsey, P., & Davies-Mostert, H. (2016). *An assessment of the economic, social and conservation value of the wildlife ranching industry and its potential to support the green economy in South Africa. Green Economy Research Report*. Johannesburg: The Endangered Wildlife Trust. Retrieved from: http://www.the-eis.com/data/literature/Taylor%20et%20al%20%202016%20An%20assessment%20of%20the%20economic%20social%20and%20conservation%20value%20of%20the%20wildlife%20ranching%20industry%20and%20its%20potential%20to%20support%20the%20green%20e.pdf
The National Agricultural Marketing Council. (2006). *Report on the investigation to identify problems for sustainable growth and development in South African wildlife ranching*. Pretoria: NAMC.
Warchol, G., & Johnson, B. (2011). Wildlife crime in the game reserves in South Africa: A research note. *International Journal of Comparative and Applied Criminal Justice, 33*(1), 143–154.
Wasser, S. K., Clark, W. J., Drori, O., Kisamo, E. S., Mailand, C., Mutayoba, B., et al. (2008). Combating the illegal trade in African elephant ivory with DNA forensics. *Conservation Biology, 22*(4), 1065–1071.
Wellsmith, M. (2011). Wildlife crime: The problems of enforcement. *European Journal on Criminal Policy and Research, 17*(2), 125–148.
Wiesner, S., Tsach, T., Belser, C., & Shor, Y. (2011). A comparative research of two lifting methods: Electrostatic lifter and gelantin lifter. *Journal of Forensic Sciences, 56*(1), 58–62.
Wilson-Wilde, L. (2010). Wildlife crime: A global problem. *Forensic Science, Medicine and Pathology, 6*, 221–222.
Wyatt, T. (2009). Exploring the organization of Russia far East's illegal wildlife trade: Two case studies of the illegal fur and illegal falcon trades. *Global Crime, 10*(1–2), 144–154.

Index

C.-H. Mayer, *Combating Wildlife Crime in South Africa*, SpringerBriefs in Criminology, https://doi.org/10.1007/978-3-030-05891-3

MIX
Papier aus verantwortungsvollen Quellen
Paper from responsible sources
FSC® C105338

If you have any concerns about our products,
you can contact us on
ProductSafety@springernature.com

In case Publisher is established outside the EU,
the EU authorized representative is:
Springer Nature Customer Service Center GmbH
Europaplatz 3, 69115 Heidelberg, Germany

Printed by Libri Plureos GmbH
in Hamburg, Germany